FIXING
HEALTHCARE

HOW EXECUTIVES CAN SAVE THEIR PEOPLE, THEIR BUSINESS, AND THE ECONOMY

DONOVAN PYLE

R^ethink

First published in Great Britain in 2025
by Rethink Press (www.rethinkpress.com)

© Copyright Donovan Pyle

Cover image © Peter Soutullo

To the American people — resilient,
creative, and ever hopeful.

Contents

Foreword

I n an industry riddled with complexity and, let's be honest, far too much smoke and mirrors, clarity is a rare and precious commodity. That's what Donovan Pyle's *Fixing Healthcare* delivers in spades. I've spent years at the Validation Institute, delving deep into the data and demanding accountability in healthcare claims, and I've seen first-hand the massive amounts of waste that permeate the system. We're talking about real money, real businesses, and the lives of real people who are affected by this waste.

What I appreciate most about Donovan's work is his unwavering commitment to transparency and his clear-eyed critique of the traditional brokerage model. Too often, we see financial incentives driving decisions, rather than the genuine best interests of employers and their employees. This book lays bare those conflicts and provides a roadmap for executives to reclaim control and make informed, strategic choices about their healthcare benefits.

Donovan doesn't just point out the problems; he offers practical solutions. He provides a strategic framework for assessing, procuring, implementing, and managing benefits in a way that puts employers back in the driver's seat. The case studies he shares are powerful examples of what's possible when you challenge the status quo and demand accountability.

At the Validation Institute, we're all about proving what works and what doesn't, using data and rigorous analysis. Donovan shares that same ethos. *Fixing Healthcare* is not about quick fixes or magic bullets. It's about understanding the fundamentals, asking the right questions, and taking a proactive, fiduciary approach to benefits management.

This book is a must-read for any executive who is tired of seeing healthcare costs spiral out of control and is ready to take concrete steps to improve their bottom line and the well-being of their employees. Donovan Pyle is a voice of reason in a noisy landscape, and his insights are invaluable. I highly recommend you heed his call to action. The stakes are too high to keep doing things the way they've always been done. It's time to fix healthcare.

Al Lewis, CEO, Validation Institute

Preface

You're losing $4,000 in profit per employee each year.

When it comes to your company's health plan, legacy brokers get paid by health insurers and make more money when your costs go up. They financially benefit from keeping you in the dark.

As a former industry insider, I've seen – and continue to see – how misaligned incentives in a misunderstood industry undermine the value and success of businesses like yours.

I wrote *Fixing Healthcare* to clarify the historical and systemic issues that created this crisis, and to empower you with the knowledge and frameworks needed to fight back and win.

Inside, you'll learn how to:

- **Uncover the "Brokerage Blind Spot":** Gain clarity on how the industry works against you.

- **Build a "Benefits Dream Team":** Create team alignment and unbiased advice.

- **Reclaim millions in profit each year:** Learn from world-class businesses that are saving money today by improving benefits and coverage.

Misaligned incentives among legacy vendors are likely costing you millions of dollars each year.

Once you see it, you can't unsee it.

By following my six-step process, you can save your company $1,000 to $4,000 per employee each year while improving benefits and coverage for your team.

Here they are:

1. Get unbiased advice: Hire your benefits architect.

   Since brokers work for insurers, you'll never reclaim this lost profit without the help of an independent management consulting firm or by bringing benefits expertise in-house.

2. Quantify your current state: Blueprint your current program.

   What gets measured gets improved. Gain new-found clarity by understanding how your company performs in the seven categories of benefits value.

3. Set goals and develop a multi-year strategy: Design your future.

   Commit to achieving measurable goals by focusing your efforts on high-value areas of your program.

4. Procure service providers: Select your expert builders.

   Find the best subcontractors by running a data-driven procurement process that forces vendors to compete on your terms.

5. Implement changes: Construct your new program.

   Collaborate with your new vendors to establish your new programs and initiatives that support your business objectives.

6. Manage and optimize: Oversee and refine.

   Measure vendor performance and continue executing on your multi-year strategy.

If you're serious about measurably improving the financial and physical health of your organization, keep reading and be sure to follow the action items listed at the end of each chapter.

Sincerely,

Donovan Pyle, CEO, Health Compass Consulting

Senior Advisor, Validation Institute

Validation Institute 2025 Benefits Advisor of the Year

Introduction

In the boardrooms of professional services firms, the floors of manufacturing plants, and the foundations of construction sites, you—the leaders and visionaries driving the American economy—are shaping our future. As chief executive officers, financial officers, and human resource officers, you expertly navigate complex landscapes, maintaining a sharp focus on talent, transparency, and trust. *Fixing Healthcare* is crafted specifically for you: the architects of innovation and the guardians of integrity in your industries. Together, we'll explore transformative strategies that resonate with your core values, empowering you to ignite a healthcare revolution and elevate your business to new heights.

As the CEO of Health Compass Consulting and a senior advisor at the Validation Institute, I draw on a wealth of expertise and a track record of innovation in the employee benefits industry. While working on both the insurer and brokerage sides of the business, I saw how their lack of transparency and financial alignment increased costs for employers and eroded trust between stakeholders. With a commitment to transparency, alignment, and results, I founded one of the nation's first fiduciary-based management consulting firms specializing in helping mid-size businesses improve how they finance and procure healthcare for employees. My approach is rooted in a proprietary process that ensures financial alignment, and this method has produced significant outcomes for organizations like the Seminole Education Association, Champion Solutions Group, and Bluewave Resource Partners.

Warren Buffett famously called healthcare a "tapeworm on the U.S. economy," and he's right. Every day, I see businesses like yours grapple with skyrocketing healthcare costs, and research shows that approximately 25% of all U.S. healthcare spending is considered waste—that's $325 billion annually, or nearly $4,000 per employee per year.[1]

Although much of this waste stems from administrative inefficiencies, pricing failures, lack of care coordination, overtreatment, and low-value care, it is the

---

1   W.H. Shrank, T.L. Rogstad, and N. Parekh, "Waste in the US
     health care system", *JAMA*, 322/15 (2019), 1501–1509, https://
     jamanetwork.com/journals/jama/article-abstract/2752664, accessed
     June 15, 2025

misaligned incentives within the benefits brokerage industry that undermine your ability to recognize and combat these forces.

In other words, many of the strategies and solutions needed to solve your organization's healthcare challenges exist, but so long as you continue relying on conflicted advice from supply-side vendors, you'll never know about them.

Fixing Healthcare emerges from this background as a profound commitment to transforming the current landscape, aiming to illuminate the often-murky waters of benefits management with transparent and actionable insights. Should the status quo remain unchanged, the repercussions extend beyond declining profit margins; they reach deep into the core of your workforce, potentially eroding the trust and confidence that your employees have in you as their leader. By addressing these challenges, we can reinforce the foundations of your business and nurture a more engaged and satisfied team.

In this book, you will uncover actionable strategies designed to transform your organization's financial health by reimagining employee benefits from a traditional cost center into a formidable strategic asset. By adopting the principles established in these chapters, you can anticipate not only a significant boost to your profitability but also the development of a competitive advantage that distinctly positions your organization ahead of others in your sector.

With each new chapter, you'll feel the stress and uncertainty usually associated with healthcare decisions dissipate. In its place, specific frameworks and practical methodologies will arm you with the clarity and confidence that are essential for making informed financial decisions. This journey focuses on improving your bottom line with quantifiable savings and productivity gains that will cultivate a vibrant and healthy workplace culture where top talent can thrive and remain committed to your organization.

Together, we will explore why most employers choose to work with external benefits firms and clarify the role these firms play. I will expose how they earn their income, including the financial misalignment this model creates, and the negative impact it's had on employers for many years.

This practice of hidden compensation and misaligned incentives is a significant contributor to the estimated $300 billion in annual waste within the U.S. employer-sponsored healthcare system.[2] It is not merely a theoretical concern; it is a documented reality. Publicly traded giants, like Aon, openly admit to

---

2   A. Bell, "CMS: U.S. employers to spend $1.3T on health benefits this year", *BenefitsPRO* (June 13, 2024), www.benefitspro. com/2024/06/13/cms-u-s-employers-to-spend-1-3t-on-health-benefits-this-year, accessed June 15, 2025

the risks of Market Derived Income (MDI) in their earnings reports, explicitly acknowledging the potential conflicts of interest stemming from "other revenue from insurance carriers."[3]

Furthermore, explosive lawsuits and class actions detail specific allegations of blatant kickbacks and concealed compensation funnelled from Pharmacy Benefit Management (PBM) organizations to Employee Benefit Consultants. Adding to this, a searing investigation by StatNews exposed the deeply entrenched and "opaque conflicts of interest" that plague prescription drug benefits, unveiling a hidden financial web between consultants and PBMs that directly inflates drug costs for employers.[4] These are glaring examples of how conflicted advice leads to disastrous purchasing decisions, forcing companies to hemorrhage money on healthcare while their most vulnerable employees suffer.

To be clear, America needs benefits professionals to help employers—and employees—maximize their return on healthcare investments, and my critique is not directed at the thousands of hardworking and

---

3   Aon plc, *Annual Report Pursuant to Section 13 or 15(d) of the Securities Exchange Act of 1934 for the Fiscal Year Ended December 31, 2020,* (United States Securities Exchange Commission, 2021), www.sec. gov/Archives/edgar/data/315293/000162828021002574/aon-20201231.htm, accessed June 15, 2025

4   B. Herman, "'It's beyond unethical': Opaque conflicts of interest permeate prescription drug benefits", *STAT* (June 20, 2023), www. statnews.com/2023/06/20/pbms-consulting-firms-investigation, accessed June 15, 2025

well-intentioned benefits professionals who strive to meet this objective. Instead, my focus is on the industry and incentive system that many of these professionals find themselves trapped in, often unconsciously and rarely with malice.

Having established that the system is not working and why, I will provide alternatives to traditional brokerage models, along with diagnostic tools and strategic roadmaps for optimizing benefits. Don't let the medical industrial complex and its army of supply-side consultants continue to extract profits from your balance sheet.

To fix the system, you must first see it.

With this guiding principle in mind, *Fixing Healthcare* will empower you with a clear understanding of employee benefits, health insurance, and the wider healthcare landscape.

America's "tapeworm" can be defeated—but only with proper guidance.

This book will arm you with the knowledge and strategies necessary to reclaim control of your healthcare spending and transform employee benefits from a burden into a strategic advantage.

If you only have time to skim through this book, I have provided you with key takeaways and action items at the end of each chapter.

Let's begin.

The power of case studies

This isn't just a theoretical discussion of systemic challenges, but an exploration of how companies just like yours have saved millions while improving care and coverage for employees.

During my tenure as a top salesperson for a multinational insurer, I observed how a small group of companies, such as trailblazing Rosen Hotels, pioneered innovative methods for financing and procuring healthcare, resulting in millions of dollars in savings while also enhancing coverage and care for employees. I wondered why more companies weren't following their lead, and naïvely thought that if I "just moved to the brokerage side of the business," I could scale these innovative solutions, help a lot of people, and make some money in the process. I soon discovered this was far from straightforward, and, as you'll see, my assumption led to some unexpected turns.

The case studies dotted throughout this book illustrate the power of unbiased advice, strategic planning, and objective benefit analysis, modeling, and scoring in action. You'll see how companies of varying sizes in different industries successfully navigated the complexities of employee benefits and succeeded, overcoming challenges and achieving significant financial and organizational improvements.

Each case study will provide a detailed examination of the specific situation, the challenges encountered, the strategies employed, and the outcomes achieved. These are learning opportunities. You'll see the obstacles, the decisions, and the processes that led to these positive outcomes. You'll understand that transformation is possible, gaining valuable insights into how these companies applied the principles I'll share. You'll discover actionable takeaways that you can apply to your own organization. Optimizing your employee benefits will save you money and empower your employees, strengthening your organization and building a sustainable future.

ONE

The Wake-Up Call
Understanding The Crisis And The Need For Change

As an executive in today's fast-paced business environment, you are constantly bombarded with distractions and competing priorities. While employee benefits may often fall to the bottom of your to-do list, consider this: healthcare costs have quietly become one of the fastest growing financial risks for businesses, often ranking among the top three expenses on profit and loss statements.

The hidden costs of healthcare

For too long, the health insurance industry has propagated the idea that "healthcare costs just go up every year, and there's not a whole lot you can do about it." This narrative, while convenient for hospitals, insurers, and legacy brokers, obscures a harsh reality: a significant portion of your healthcare spending is simply being wasted.

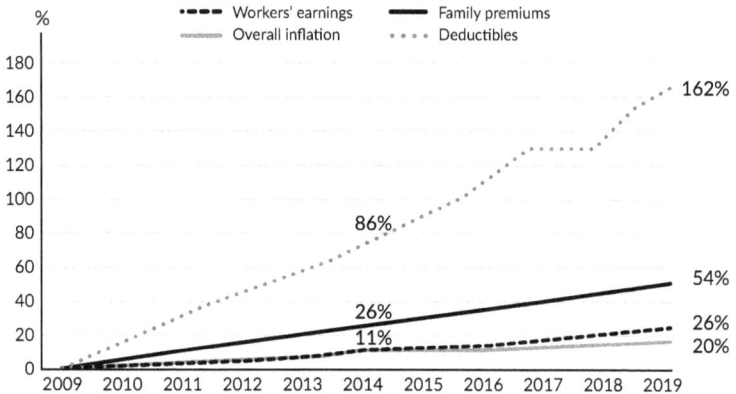

Premiums and deductibles rise faster than workers' wages over past decade. Source: KFF Employer Health Benefits Survey, 2018–2019; Kaiser HRET Survey of Employer-Sponsored Health Benefits, 2009–2017; Bureau of Labor Statistics Consumer Price Index, U.S. City Average of Annual Inflation (April to April), 2009–2019; Bureau of Labor Statistics, Seasonally Adjusted Data from the Current Employment Statistics Survey, 2009–2019 (April to April)

I've already shared the staggering research from the *Journal of the American Medical Association* (JAMA) revealing that an estimated 25% of all healthcare spending in the U.S. is considered waste.[5] In 2024, U.S. employers spent an estimated $1.3 trillion on

---

5   W.H. Shrank, T.L. Rogstad, and N. Parekh, "Waste in the US health care system", *JAMA*, 322/15 (2019), 1501–1509, https://jamanetwork.com/journals/jama/article-abstract/2752664, accessed June 15, 2025

healthcare, which means that approximately $325 billion was wasted. Since employers covered around 82 million employees that year, the average employer overpaid for healthcare and health insurance by roughly $4,000 per employee in 2024.[6]

Imagine what your company could do with an extra $1,000 or $2,000 per employee each year, let alone the full projected $4,000. This money could be reinvested in sales, marketing, employee raises, new equipment, research and development, or simply bolstering your bottom line. The $325 billion waste is not a minor inefficiency; it's a massive drain on our economy and it needs to be stopped.

Impact on business competitiveness and growth

Navigating the healthcare benefits industry is incredibly complex, and it's important to understand that many of these complexities are by design. It's perfectly normal to seek outside specialized expertise, just as you might consult with CPAs or lawyers. However, the challenge in healthcare benefits is unique. Businesses often rely on brokers for guidance, but as we will discuss in the following chapter, these

---

6   G. Claxton, M. Rae, and A. Winger, *Employer-Sponsored Health Insurance 101* (KFF, 2024), www.kff.org/health-policy-101-employer-sponsored-health-insurance/?entry=table-of-contents-who-is-covered-by-employer-sponsored-health-insurance, accessed June 15, 2025

brokers primarily work for and are compensated by insurance companies, not the employers themselves. This inherent conflict of interest makes the healthcare benefits space particularly difficult to navigate and manage effectively. Therefore, the current state of affairs is often a consequence of this system's inherent intricacies, not necessarily a reflection on you or your team's lack of diligence.

Beyond the direct financial losses, the negative impact of waste includes reduced competitiveness, stifled growth, employee morale and retention, personal liability, and employee health. The stark reality is that, by failing to address the hidden waste and misaligned incentives, you are throwing money away and allowing your resources to be siphoned off by an opaque system that profits from unnecessary complexity— and your ignorance.

The cost of inaction is not just financial; it's about the missed opportunity to empower your employees, enhance their well-being, and foster a more competitive and sustainable business. By taking a proactive approach and demanding clarity and control, you can reclaim those wasted dollars and transform your healthcare benefits program from a cost center into a strategic asset.

This is about trimming the fat and building muscle. When we talk about healthcare reform, we're not just talking about saving money—we're talking about economic empowerment. Financial waste in health-care hinders growth, employee satisfaction, and your employees' ability to pursue their dreams.

Why this matters: A personal note

In October of 2018, I was unexpectedly fired from a large employee benefits brokerage firm for advocating on behalf of my clients. The termination was odd because:

1. I was a contract employee who received no base salary or benefits.
2. I was generating good revenue for the firm.
3. I believed my role was to serve as a fiduciary, protecting clients from the conflicting financial interests of insurance companies and other vendors.

I was wrong.

During my termination, I was told that, despite my revenue production, I was being too "hard" on a specific insurer who, coincidentally, paid them their largest bonus each year.

I was devastated.

My entire motivation for transitioning from the insurer side of the business to the brokerage side was to help employers avoid overpaying for health insurance, a financial product whose inflation rate was eroding corporate margins and hindering many Americans' ability to achieve economic stability.

However, I was naïve and didn't fully grasp how the revenue streams between health insurers and benefits brokers impacted the latter's relationship with employers.

During my tenure as a top sales representative for an insurer, benefits brokers were my primary clients. Although I was effective at selling the company's products, I was often dumbfounded by the number of brokers who, frankly, seemed apathetic about recommending the best solutions to employers. After all, don't employers use benefits brokers to help them get the most value for their money?

That's not the way the industry worked.

In the year leading up to my termination, I had been inspired by David Contorno, who—after spending years at a brokerage firm—developed what may have been the first fee-based benefits consulting firm, E-Powered Benefits. David understood that accepting compensation from vendors would undermine his ability to give clients unbiased advice on how to maximize the return on their benefits investments, and this was the genesis of his decision to go out on his own. After my termination, I not only wanted to save face, but I absolutely needed to provide for my family. Within a week, I followed Contorno's lead and founded my management consulting firm, Health Compass Consulting.

I had no idea what I was in for. Still, I knew that if I didn't accept commissions or bonuses from health insurers and their affiliated vendors, I would be free to provide my clients with unbiased advice on how to improve the financial and physical health of their organizations.

My journey began with a single client and a severely broken ankle resulting from the major renovations my wife, Emily, and I were doing on our dream house that year. Although my broken ankle brought our home renovation to a standstill, it allowed me to pour energy into my new business.

But wait, there's more…

Just two weeks after the titanium rod and pins were surgically installed in my right ankle, Emily and I discovered that she was pregnant with our first child.

That moment felt like utter chaos. Heat exhaustion, a shattered ankle, a house in shambles, and a new business were a terrifying ordeal. Amid that chaos, Emily and I were also buzzing with excitement about the prospect of being parents, and our only option was an almost inhuman level of focus. In an unexpected twist, the injury forced me to dedicate every ounce of energy to ensuring that my new business and client were a success.

During my client's 2019 benefits renewal, we removed all commissions from their health plan, replaced it with a transparent flat fee, and developed a contract outlining our scope of services. I also included a clause in the contract that stated that 100% of any bonuses paid by vendors to me associated with the health plan would be remitted back to the client within ninety days.

Although I didn't fully recognize it at the time, Health Compass Consulting moved me out of the business of selling health insurance and into the business of selling advisory services. With a newfound sense of freedom, I was able to analyze a much wider range of health insurance products and show my first, and only, client how they compared and what the short- and long-term ramifications of each would be. I was also able to procure a variety of partially self-funded models in which my client would purchase less insurance and have more money to spend on healthcare itself. After educating their executive team, they decided to implement a custom solution, which eliminated waste and ultimately saved them $3,026 per employee, while improving network access and coverage. It was a solid win all round. Can you imagine if every company in the U.S. spent $3,026 less per employee each year on health insurance and had better coverage?

Companies could attract and retain better talent. Businesses could enjoy higher valuations. Shareholders could earn higher dividends. School teachers would enjoy higher salaries. Municipalities would have less pressure to raise taxes on citizens.

On… and on.

From a benefits perspective, the results my first client achieved were only made possible because I was free to give them unbiased advice. Unlike brokerage firms, I wasn't going to work on commissions and make more money when my client's health insurance costs went up. I wasn't going to make money in bonuses for recommending one health insurer over another. I was free to give employers unbiased advice that helped them maximize the return on their benefits investments, plain and simple.

Fixing Healthcare began its life as a personal story. By shining a light on the healthcare and health insurance industry's broken landscape, my goal is to empower you with the clarity and frameworks needed to improve the financial and physical health of your organization.

CASE STUDY: Rosen Hotels—A blueprint for fixing healthcare

This case study explores how Harris Rosen, founder of Rosen Hotels, revolutionized healthcare for his employees, resulting in significant cost savings, improved employee well-being, and unexpected community benefits. His approach offers a valuable model for executives seeking to address healthcare challenges within their own organizations.

Rosen's initial frustration with healthcare costs

In 1974, Harris Rosen bootstrapped Rosen Hotels, which would grow into a successful chain throughout Central Florida. However, like many business owners, Rosen was dissatisfied with the rising cost of healthcare. As he stated in a 2021 interview on the Reconstructing Healthcare podcast, "We were handling our healthcare and life insurance pretty much the same as everyone else... and I wasn't really happy with our annual payments."[7] Despite having low claims in 1990, Rosen was informed that his premiums would increase due to losses in the insurer's broader risk pool.

The epiphany and the birth of Rosen Care

This news sparked an epiphany. Rosen realized he needed to take a more proactive approach. Consequently, he terminated his traditional health insurance policy and began negotiating directly with healthcare providers in the Orlando area. This led to two key initiatives: Rosen established an on-site clinic by employing a primary care physician, and he negotiated a risk-sharing agreement with a local

---

7   M. Menairi, "Episode 78: Harris Rosen and Ashley Bacot", Reconstructing Healthcare (2021), https://podcasts.apple.com/us/podcast/reconstructing-healthcare-innovative-solutions-for/id1240066325, accessed June 15, 2025

hospital. This set the foundation for what would later be dubbed "Rosen Care."

Dramatic cost reduction and program success

Rosen explained, "The first year was absolutely amazing... our costs declined from ~$1,100 per covered life to ~$750. *Trend* magazine in Central Florida put me on the cover and called our program 'Rosen Care'... that was the beginning." Since its inception in 1991, Rosen Care has saved the company over $500 million on healthcare while providing a superior health plan for its employees.[8] This demonstrates the potential for significant cost savings through innovative healthcare management.

Key to success: Removing barriers and enhancing access

According to Ashley Bacot, long-time director of Rosen Care, "the more barriers we removed from the program, the more access, the better quality, the better service, the lower costs we produced."[9] Bacot continued, "When our associates say there's a barrier, we remove it... Our costs are about half what our competitors pay, and our benefits are much richer. We don't have any deductibles or coinsurance, and 90% of our prescription drugs are free." This emphasis on removing

---

8   Rosen Hotels & Resorts, *RosenCare and PeopleOne Health Join Forces to Transform Healthcare Market in Florida* (2024), www.rosenhotels.com/rosencare-and-peopleone-health-join-forces-to-transform-healthcare-market-in-florida, accessed June 15, 2025

9   M. Menairi, "Episode 78: Harris Rosen and Ashley Bacot", Reconstructing Healthcare (2021), https://podcasts.apple.com/us/podcast/reconstructing-healthcare-innovative-solutions-for/id1240066325, accessed June 15, 2025

obstacles to care and enhancing access was central to the program's success.

Healthier employees, lower costs

Rosen later stated a fundamental principle: "If you keep people healthy, you will reduce healthcare costs." This philosophy underscores the importance of preventive care and proactive health management.

Impact on employee turnover

One of the unexpected benefits of Rosen Care was a significant reduction in employee turnover. Rosen noted, "Turnover in hospitality and restaurants is pretty dramatic... probably 50% to 70%. Rosen has been in the low single digits for many years." This highlights how excellent healthcare benefits can contribute to a more stable and satisfied workforce.

Philanthropy: Extending the benefits beyond Rosen Hotels

The financial gains achieved through Rosen Care enabled Rosen to engage in significant philanthropic efforts. He "adopted" the Tangelo Park community in Central Florida in 1993, providing funding for preschool education.[10] This program expanded into the Parramore community, including the construction of a preschool and the provision of college scholarships. "That's my way of saying 'thank you, God,'" Rosen stated. "All of this was made possible because of the success we've had with our little company."

---

10 "Harris Rosen", *Wikipedia: The Free Encyclopedia*, Wikimedia Foundation, July 13, 2024, https://en.wikipedia.org/wiki/Harris_Rosen, accessed June 15, 2025

Legacy and call to action

Harris Rosen passed away during the writing of this book, in November 2024, but his pioneering work in healthcare and employee benefits inspired me and countless others to explore and scale similar solutions.

As fiduciaries of your organization's health and prosperity, consider Rosen's innovative approach not just as a success story, but as a clarion call: re-examine your current healthcare strategies, embrace transparency, demand accountability, and unlock the full potential of a truly strategic asset—your people.

Key takeaways

- Healthcare costs are a major financial risk for businesses.

- The average employer is overpaying for care by around $4,000 per employee, per year.

- This waste impacts business competitiveness, growth, and employee morale.

- Misaligned incentives within the legacy brokerage industry keep you in the dark and perpetuate this waste.

Action items

- Consider what your company would do with an additional $1,000 to $4,000 per employee per year of interest-free working capital.

- Consider the impact of rising healthcare costs on employee well-being and retention.

TWO

How We Got Here
The Story Of Healthcare

As a professional, you'll be fascinated to discover the history of healthcare in the U.S., and you may even apply some of its lessons to your own organization and industry.

Fueled by the lobbying efforts of unions, government interventions, and an unquenchable thirst for profits, the industry became neither government-dominated nor market-driven. Instead, it was an economic freak whose landscape is perpetually distorted by government interventions, resulting in unintended consequences, mystery, and misaligned incentives between stakeholders.

Similar to the housing market's bubble and eventual collapse in 2008, the health insurance and medical industrial complex has become an opaque system that thrives on complexity. This complexity obscures the true costs and underlying dynamics, making it difficult for employers and individuals to navigate. While not necessarily driven by malicious intent, it's clear that the current system is designed to perpetuate itself.

An early history of U.S. healthcare

In 1900, the average American citizen spent just $5 on healthcare a year (~1% of their income).[11] This was generally affordable, so there was no need for health insurance. Before the 1900s, hospitals were merely places where the indigent went to comfort themselves in their last days, and people rarely sought medical care. Given their role at the turn of the century, the healthcare provider's mantra was "to cure seldom, to help sometimes, and to comfort always."[12] Hardly the foundations of a multitrillion-dollar industry.

Given that the U.S. healthcare system was largely ineffective and inexpensive in its early days, most

---

11   A. Blumberg and A. Davidson, *Accidents of History Created U.S. Health System* (NPR, 2009), www.npr.org/2009/10/22/114045132/accidents-of-history-created-u-s-health-system, accessed June 15, 2025

12   Institute of Medicine Committee on Employment-Based Health Benefits, "Origins and evolution of employment-based health benefits", in M.J. Field, and H.T. Shapiro (eds), *Employment and Health Benefits: A Connection at Risk* (National Academies Press, 1993), available at: www.ncbi.nlm.nih.gov/books/NBK235989, accessed June 15, 2025

Americans were not concerned about the price of healthcare. Instead, American workers aimed to protect their income with disability insurance, as worksite accidents were common in those days. As a result, some forward-thinking employers in the early 1900s contracted directly with physicians to care for employees who had been injured on the job. This approach aimed to facilitate faster healing so that employees could return to work as quickly as possible.[13]

When legislators from President Theodore Roosevelt's Progressive Party suggested a national health insurance plan in 1917, it faced fierce opposition from the American Medical Association (AMA) and caused one New York physician to say "Nowhere has the swinish greed of the debasing propaganda of state socialism been more brazenly exposed than in this merciless attempt to steal the livelihood of the most unselfish profession in the world."[14]

Between opposition from the AMA and the trend toward Federalism, these early efforts to implement government-sponsored health insurance largely failed.

Medical advancements, however, continued to move forward at an accelerated pace. The effects of medical research, physician education, immunization,

---

13 Ibid
14 Ibid

sterilization, and other measures, resulted in better health outcomes, increased operating expenses, and rising prices for patients. While hospitals attempted to market themselves as capable of delivering happier outcomes, consumers remained skeptical and continued to spend more on cosmetic goods than on healthcare throughout the 1900s.

The status quo seemed to suit everyone until the Great Depression. The economic crash hit hospitals particularly hard, and to remedy this, executives at Baylor University Medical Center in Dallas had an idea. What if they could convince employers to pre-pay for their services via a subscription plan so that patients would be less apprehensive about going to the hospital for care, and the hospital's cash flow could stabilize? In 1929, the hospital entered into an agreement with the Dallas Teachers' Union, allowing teachers to pre-pay $0.50 a month in exchange for "free" admission and services at Baylor Hospital. The business model was a success.

By 1934, the nonprofit plan became known as "Blue Cross," and its success quickly caught the attention of hospitals across the country that were seeking to stabilize their finances. Here's the fascinating part: in addition to funding from foundations and loans, hospitals themselves invested in the creation of fourteen additional Blue Cross plans across eleven states by 1940. This was not merely an outside entity; hospitals strategically built these insurance plans as a distribution mechanism to ensure a more predictable patient and cash flow.

While the modern media would like us to think that hospitals and health insurers have an adversarial relationship and sit on opposite sides of the "table," it's important to remember that hospitals invested in creating health insurers for distribution purposes. Absent the ability to pre-pay for hospital services via the construction of risk pools and other financing mechanisms, patients would rarely be able to afford hospital services.

Hospitals played a significant role in the development and promotion of such products, and some large employers offered these plans to employees, who, interestingly, paid 100% of the premiums themselves. By 1940, over six million Americans had quietly enrolled in Blue Cross plans throughout the country.

NOTE

Payments for physician services such as pathology, radiology, and anesthesiology were excluded from hospital payments. For the most part, this division, dating from the Blue Cross days, still exists in U.S. healthcare today.

These early insurers allocated most of their resources toward developing and administering insurance products, as well as obtaining approval for their distribution at the state level. Since each state has its own approval process, this was—and continues to be—no small feat.

During the 1930s, various individual health insurance products were introduced, primarily distributed by door-to-door agents hired by the insurer, who earned a commission for each sale. To solicit the sale of a policy, these agents were responsible for "field underwriting," meaning that they were required to capture health information from proposed insureds and work up a proposal with pricing, terms, and conditions for the prospect's consideration.

The process of field underwriting was so crucial that, in 1930, the industry's first trade association aptly named itself the National Association of Health Underwriters (NAHU). As the number of insurers and group products increased, so grew the need for underwriters in the field.

NOTE

To more accurately reflect the changing demographics of its members and their roles, NAHU rebranded as the National Association of Benefits and Insurance Professionals (NABIP) in 2023.

For insurers, the task of growing and maintaining in-house distribution channels became more challenging in 1938 when federal minimum-wage requirements went into effect.

Since most sales teams worked on commissions and received no base salary, minimum-wage laws created a problem: how could insurers afford to pay agents whose performance and payable commissions fell below the required minimum wage?

To mitigate this financial risk, most insurers transitioned their in-house sales agents to independent contractors. One byproduct of this change, perhaps unforeseen by insurers, was that these independent sales agents would now be able to offer and sell products from multiple insurers, not just their own.

The process of getting "appointed" by a carrier gave brokers the authority to sell and service the insurer's products to consumers whose demand for such products was increasing.

This change marked the beginning of the brokerage industry, which would solidify itself as the dominant retail distribution partner for health insurers and, by proxy, hospitals.

The early landscape of U.S. healthcare was a far cry from the complex system we navigate today. From minimal spending and a focus on accidents and illnesses to the gradual emergence of hospitals, pre-paid plans, and the initial push for national insurance, the seeds of our current structure were sown. However, these early developments, driven by necessity and reacting to economic shifts, laid the groundwork for a system that would soon be reshaped by larger forces. The coming decades, particularly the interventions during and after World War II, would fundamentally transform how employers and employees interacted with healthcare, ultimately shaping the modern employee benefits industry as we know it.

Why employers offer benefits

During WWII, 16 million working-age Americans were taken out of the labor market to support the war effort. The decreased labor supply resulted in higher wages and inflation that shocked both legislators and citizens. To combat these inflationary pressures, the government passed the Stabilization Act of 1942, which immediately froze wages for 60 million Americans. As part of the deal, unions accepted a halt on pay raises but negotiated that employer contributions towards pensions and welfare plans could still rise, excluded from wages. It proved to be a decisive move. Wartime employers promptly introduced tax-advantaged benefits programs to attract and retain talent, and this resulted in a tripling of participation in group health plans by 1948.[15]

---

15   Institute of Medicine Committee on Employment-Based Health Benefits, "Origins and evolution of employment-based health benefits", in M.J. Field, and H.T. Shapiro (eds), *Employment and Health Benefits: A Connection at Risk* (National Academies Press, 1993), available at: www.ncbi.nlm.nih.gov/books/NBK235989, accessed June 15, 2025

> **NOTE**
>
> In 1948, court cases involving the Inland Steel Company and the United Steel Workers resulted in federal laws requiring employers to collectively bargain over employee pensions and health plans. For the following two years, nearly half of all union strikes were related to benefits issues. By 1958, 36 million workers were enrolled in health plans that had been collectively bargained and, overall, 123 million Americans had some form of private health coverage.[16]

As demand for group benefits grew from both employers and employees, so did the number of insurers. By 1960, approximately 700 different insurers were in the market, selling individual and group products. This lies in stark contrast to 2025, where a handful of publicly traded insurers dominate the fully insured market and a few dozen reinsurers provide "stop loss" insurance for level-funded and partially self-funded employer plans.

It's crucial to recognize that, in 2014, the Affordable Care Act (ACA) further cemented the employer's role in providing healthcare. By mandating that "large employers" (those with more than fifty employees) offer "credible" healthcare coverage, the ACA reinforced a system deeply rooted in wartime policy

---

16   Ibid

decisions. As of the time of writing, there is little political support for repealing the employer mandate and, thus, stakeholders must accept and navigate the playing field as it is, not how we wish it were.

The conditions forged during WWII fundamentally altered the landscape and industries' relationship with the labor force. What began as a wartime measure to stabilize inflation evolved into a cornerstone of American employment, shaping expectations and becoming deeply embedded in our economic fabric. The decisions made in those dark days have had a lasting impact, and U.S. employers now spend $1.3 trillion to cover approximately 165 million Americans with healthcare benefits each year.

Navigating today's healthcare benefits industry is incredibly complex, and it's important to understand that many of these complexities are by design. It's perfectly normal for executives, benefits managers, and HR professionals to seek outside specialized expertise, just as they might consult with CPAs or lawyers. However, the challenge in healthcare benefits is unique.

Businesses often rely on brokers for guidance, but brokers primarily work for and are compensated by insurance companies, not the employers themselves. This inherent conflict of interest makes the healthcare benefits space particularly difficult to navigate and manage effectively. The current state of affairs is a consequence of the system's inherent intricacies, not necessarily a reflection on you or your team's lack of diligence.

Regardless, the status quo in healthcare benefits is unsustainable, and continuing to accept rising costs, opaque pricing, and conflicted advice is not only financially irresponsible, it's a missed opportunity for economic growth.

Before we move on to the solutions, I'd like to inspire you by sharing a case study from my colleague, Justin Leader, that demonstrates how unbiased advice can save employers millions.

CASE STUDY: Uncovering hidden costs that waste millions

In the intricate world of healthcare benefits, employers often find themselves navigating a complex maze of costs, regulations, and hidden fees. The story of a 600-employee pharmaceutical manufacturer serves as a powerful example of how expert fiduciary guidance can uncover significant issues and lead to substantial savings. This organization, spending a considerable $14 million annually on medical and prescription drug costs through a fully insured plan, believed they were operating under a fee-based agreement with their broker. However, a deeper investigation by the fiduciary-based consulting firm BenefitsDNA, led by Justin Leader, revealed a starkly different reality.

Upon engaging with BenefitsDNA, the manufacturer began to understand the importance of their fiduciary duties and the need for complete transparency. At BenefitsDNA's recommendation, the manufacturer requested an ERISA 408(b)(2) compensation disclosure, a critical step in understanding broker compensation structures. What this disclosure revealed was eye-opening: the broker was earning an additional $200,000 in indirect compensation through overrides and commissions from the insurer, in addition to the $200,000 annual fee the employer believed they were paying. This discovery highlighted a clear misalignment of incentives, where the broker's financial interests were not fully aligned with those of the employer.

The lack of transparency extended beyond compensation. The incumbent broker had withheld the renewal information, preventing the employer from assessing cost changes. When the renewal was finally disclosed, it came with a staggering 50% increase, amounting to an additional $7 million. The employer had no access to the data justifying this exorbitant increase. BenefitsDNA recognized this as a serious issue, indicative of potential fiduciary breaches and a lack of accountability.

Further investigation by the firm uncovered violations of transparency rules and the concealment of rebates. The carrier had attested to the federal government that no gag clauses were present in their contract, yet the employer was denied meaningful access to claims data and cost breakdowns. When BenefitsDNA intervened and requested RxDC reporting, which should disclose rebate details, the carrier initially refused to comply. This refusal raised significant red flags, especially considering the group spent $5 million on prescription drugs, and BenefitsDNA estimated that $1–$2 million in rebates were unaccounted for within the carrier's reported Medical Loss Ratio (MLR).

Through three weeks of diligent negotiations and persistent demands for transparency, a remarkable turnaround was achieved. After terminating their broker and hiring BenefitsDNA for a flat annual fee, the firm successfully negotiated the full elimination of the 50% premium increase, saving the client $7 million.

This case underscores several key issues, highlighting the value of working with a fiduciary-based management consulting firm:

1. **Unbiased advice should be non-negotiable.** Engaging a fiduciary-based firm provided the employer with the expertise and guidance needed to uncover hidden compensation and demand transparency.

2. **You need data transparency.** With BenefitsDNA's guidance, the plan sponsor insisted on access to claims data, rebates, and renewal justifications, revealing significant issues.

3. **Carrier accountability is essential.** A proactive approach ensured that the carrier was held accountable for providing accurate reporting and cost breakdowns.

4. **You must eliminate misaligned incentives.** BenefitsDNA's fully transparent consulting

arrangement prevented the employer from incurring millions in unnecessary costs and aligned their interests with the employer's.

This case study is a testament to the power of working with fiduciary-based management consulting firms. By prioritizing fiduciary responsibility, demanding transparency, and aligning incentives, the 600-employee pharmaceutical company was able to reduce waste, achieve significant cost savings, and ensure the employer was maximizing the value of their benefits investments.

Key takeaways

- Hospitals created health insurers for distribution purposes.

- Health insurers created the brokerage industry for the retail distribution of their products.

Action items

- Recognize that hospitals, insurers, and legacy brokers financially benefit from rising prices—at your expense.

THREE

Brokers And The Great Misalignment

A s we have already seen, U.S. employers spend approximately $1.3 trillion each year on healthcare, of which *The Journal of the American Medical Association* (JAMA) estimates 25% is wasted.[17] This waste is a real drain on company resources, and a significant portion of it stems from the great misalignment I am about to explore.

From 1900 to 2023, Americans went from spending ~1% to ~15% of their gross annual income on healthcare and health insurance, and in 2024, it cost

---

17 W.H. Shrank, T.L. Rogstad, and N. Parekh, "Waste in the US health care system", *JAMA*, 322/15 (2019), 1501–1509, https://jamanetwork.com/journals/jama/article-abstract/2752664, accessed June 15, 2025

employers an average of $25,572 to cover families enrolled in their plans.[18]

In 1929, Baylor University Hospital and the Dallas Teachers' Union's Blue Cross Plan created a profitable business model that allowed hospitals to better serve working populations. Similar to how the software-as-a-service (SaaS) model improved the cash flows of technology companies, the hospital-as-a-service model, invented by Baylor, resulted in more predictable cash flows for hospitals, enabling them to remain open throughout the Great Depression.

Baylor's success sparked an influx of capital from hospitals and outside investors, and by 1942, the newly minted "health insurers" became the dominant distribution partners for hospitals.

Insurers developed in-house sales teams for retail distribution, and customers were found in the door-to-door fashion that was common at the time. When Federal minimum-wage laws went into effect, many insurers were concerned about having to pay a minimum wage to underperforming salespeople. To avoid this risk, most insurers transitioned their sales forces

---

18 KFF news release, "Annual family premiums for employer coverage rise 7% to average $25,572 in 2024, benchmark survey finds, after also rising 7% last year" (KFF, 2024), www.kff.org/health-costs/press-release/annual-family-premiums-for-employer-coverage-rise-7-to-average-25572-in-2024-benchmark-survey-finds-after-also-rising-7-last-year, accessed June 15, 2025

to independent contractors, marking the dawn of the brokerage industry.

Instead of just selling one insurer's products, these new independent agents could sell products from multiple insurers.

The growth of independent salespeople

The expansion of independent insurance salespeople marked a significant shift in the industry. As more salespeople transitioned to independent contractor status, they gained the ability to offer products from various insurers, thus collecting commissions from multiple sources. While some insurance companies maintained in-house "captive" sales teams, which restricted agents to selling only their products, the "independent" distribution channels experienced rapid growth. This shift offered a perceived benefit to both insurers (supply) seeking wider distribution, and employers/consumers (demand) seeking choice.

In theory, this transformation positioned independent contractors as more than mere salespeople. Instead of simply pushing a single product, they presented themselves as "consultants," authorized to offer a variety of options. No longer confined to a single insurer's portfolio, these contractors could access, recommend, and sell a diverse range of insurance products to employers. Their pitch centered on matching clients with the most suitable health insurance solutions, effectively launching the modern employee benefits brokerage industry.

The concept of "independence" held significant appeal, leading to the establishment of comprehensive benefits firms. These firms developed their own sales and service teams, proudly advertising their capacity to offer products from numerous insurers. As their primary goal was to expand their client base by selling directly to employers and consumers, these brokerage firms rapidly became the dominant and preferred distribution partners for insurers across many regions.

This division of labor allowed insurers to focus on their core competencies, which included product development, claim adjudication, and expanding into new markets by navigating each state's product approval process. For employers, brokers provided valuable procurement services in that they could obtain proposals (aka "quotes") from a wide range of health insurers, help them understand the terms and conditions of each product, and provide recommendations about which products would best support the employer's objectives. Additionally, brokers could act as a conduit between employers, employees, patients, and insurers when claims and billing disputes arose.

Because insurance companies compensated brokers for selling their products, brokers typically didn't charge employers directly for their services, and this made it easy for employers to engage with them. Since the insurance companies were covering the cost, employers could receive product recommendations and advice from brokers without paying the professional fees normally associated with hiring outside attorneys, financial advisors, or accountants. At the time, the arrangement seemed like a win-win for everyone involved.

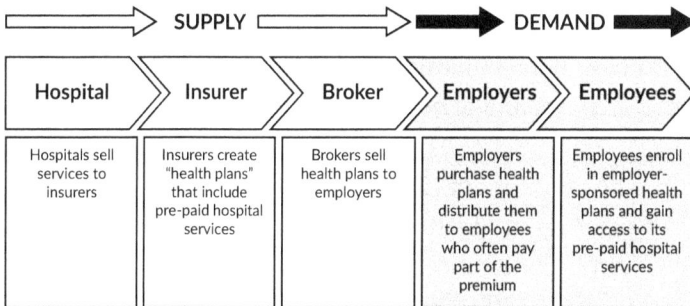

⟹ SUPPLY ⟹ ⟹ DEMAND ⟹				
Hospital	Insurer	Broker	Employers	Employees
Hospitals sell services to insurers	Insurers create "health plans" that include pre-paid hospital services	Brokers sell health plans to employers	Employers purchase health plans and distribute them to employees who often pay part of the premium	Employees enroll in employer-sponsored health plans and gain access to its pre-paid hospital services

Hospital distribution channel

No such thing as free

As is often the case, the concept of "free" is often an illusion. Services do come at a cost. While the scope and value of benefits brokers are not always clear, most businesses expect their brokers to help them maximize the return on their benefits investments. In other words, they help you get the most value for your money.

In 2015, Health Rosetta co-founder Dave Chase noted: "Having spoken to over 100 employers last year, it's become clear to me that they defer most benefits decisions to their benefits consultant, and no one has a bigger influence over health purchasing than benefits consultants from Alliant, Aon Hewitt, HUB International, Mercer, Willis Towers Watson, USI, and many regional players."

Since most executives have little or no technical expertise in the complex world of healthcare financing and procurement, about 81% of employers rely on benefits professionals—mainly brokers—to procure, implement, and manage benefits programs on their behalf.[19]

In the winter of 2013, I attended the National Association of Health Underwriters' (NAHU) annual "Capitol Conference." Each year, some of our trade association's 100,000 members travel to Washington, D.C., to advocate for employers, patients, and the insurance industry by educating legislators on areas we believe can be improved through regulation and deregulation.

The Affordable Care Act (ACA), regarded as the most significant healthcare legislation since the introduction of Medicare in 1965, was passed in 2010 and was set to be fully implemented in 2014. As we approached this

---

19 MetLife, *The Trust Imperative: New strategies to accelerate talent outcomes for a changing workforce* (U.S. Employee Benefit Trends Study, 2025), www.metlife.com/workforce-insights, accessed September 18, 2025

looming legislation, the atmosphere among our members was somber—like mourning the loss of someone who died too young.

Given the monumental changes the ACA was about to impose on the private sector, many brokers who attended the D.C. conference that year were fearful. Would small businesses stop offering health insurance to employees, and would this mark the end of the brokerage industry? While some industry veterans contemplated retirement, others considered joining larger firms, and others completely revamped their practices to accommodate expected growth in the individual market.

NOTE

The health and welfare side of the insurance industry is divided into two camps: the "individual" market, whose products are intended for consumers, and the "group" market, whose products are built for employers.

The ACA placed significant responsibilities on many employers, creating challenges that persist to this day. Under the ACA, these employers must provide adequate health coverage to at least 95% of their eligible workforce and their dependents. This coverage must also be considered affordable, meaning that the employer needs to contribute to the premiums so that employees' costs for the lowest-priced plan remain reasonable. Additionally, plans must offer minimum essential benefits, including basic preventive services at no out-of-pocket cost to employees. Failing to meet these requirements can result in substantial penalties from the IRS.

While it seems obvious now, at the time, few predicted that the ACA—with its thousands of pages of nuance—would serve as an opportunity for brokers to increase the value they could provide to employers who needed help understanding the law's new requirements.

As you well know, companies regularly outsource certain functions to experts in a particular field because it allows them to streamline operations, reduce costs, and gain access to specialized expertise. More importantly, by outsourcing these tasks, companies can focus on their core competencies and avoid the cost of hiring and managing in-house staff.

Similarly, companies often outsource the oversight of their employee benefits programs to benefits firms (again, often brokers) who may possess specialized knowledge and experience in navigating complex regulations, negotiating with insurance carriers, and optimizing benefit plans. While larger organizations can afford to develop in-house benefits teams, the vast majority of businesses still supplement internal teams with the help of external benefits professionals.

From a distance, it's tempting to think that employee benefits brokers simply sell insurance products to employers and enroll employees in those products during the "open enrollment" period. While this is true in some cases, the reality is that most employers desperately need services that go way beyond the mere transaction of purchasing insurance. As market conditions have changed, the role that benefits firms play is evolving, and many of them find it difficult to articulate exactly what they do.

There are good reasons why this lack of clarity persists: benefits brokers (the dominant form of benefits firms) get paid by—and work for—insurance companies. They are distribution partners for health insurers and, therefore, get paid to sell insurance.

However, as regulatory requirements for employers have become more complex, plan designs have become more intricate, and technology has influenced how employers manage employee data, the role of benefits firms and brokers has moved way beyond simply selling products. Many employers expect brokers to help them maximize the return on their benefits investments through benefits consulting, procurement, and the overall management of their programs.

As we're about to uncover, the disconnect between what employers expect from benefits brokers and what's delivered is at the heart of why healthcare has become a top expense for many businesses.

The brokerage blind spot: Unveiling hidden conflicts

We have established that U.S. businesses are wasting approximately $325 billion annually on healthcare, and a significant contributor to this waste stems from the inherent conflicts of interest within the legacy benefits brokerage model.

By illustrating how the benefits industry and its misaligned incentives were established, my goal is to equip you with the confidence, clarity, and control necessary to improve the financial and physical health of your organization, and by extension, your community.

For employers who rely on legacy brokers to recommend which products to buy (if any), a revenue model based on commissions and bonuses paid by insurers to brokers creates a significant conflict of interest. A brokerage firm's income is directly tied to the volume and types of insurance products it recommends and sells. As David Smith, Senior Vice President at Eben Concepts, notes, "Nearly every large agency is driven by revenue rather than outcomes for their clients."

A 2018 ProPublica investigation by the late Marshall Allen revealed a web of hidden commissions, bonus incentives, and preferred partner programs that often steered employers toward specific plans, regardless of their actual suitability.[20]

Large publicly traded giants like Aon attempt to obscure blatant kickbacks from insurers and pharmacy benefits managers by deceptively labeling them Market Derived Income, or MDI, in their quarterly earnings reports. This is a calculated effort to hide the risks and inherent conflicts of interest created by these pernicious revenue streams. Recent lawsuits against companies like Wells Fargo, along with investigations by StatNews exposing the "opaque conflicts of interest" in prescription drug benefits, reveal the harsh reality: this pervasive problem of conflicted advice leads to disastrous purchasing decisions and massive financial losses for employers.[21]

The bottom line is that, when a broker's income is tied to selling specific products, their advice may be unintentionally biased. This bias can lead to employers overpaying for insurance, receiving inadequate coverage, missing out on innovative solutions, or simply buying products they don't need.

---

20 M. Allen "Why your health insurer doesn't care about your big bills", *ProPublica* (May 25, 2018), www.propublica.org/article/why-your-health-insurer-does-not-care-about-your-big-bills, accessed June 15, 2025

21 B. Herman, "'It's beyond unethical': Opaque conflicts of interest permeate prescription drug benefits", *STAT* (June 20, 2023), www.statnews.com/2023/06/20/pbms-consulting-firms-investigation, accessed June 15, 2025

While the value proposition created by benefits brokers is important and well intended, the challenge is that benefits brokers are paid by the same entities that employers expect them to negotiate with on their behalf: health insurers. The relationship between stakeholders in the supply chain, their business models, and financial incentives skews results in one direction—and it's not towards employers, employees, or their families.

To address these conflicts of interest, the Consolidated Appropriations Act (CAA) of 2021 introduced important transparency rules. These regulations require brokers to disclose all forms of compensation received, both "direct" and "indirect," allowing employers to be fully aware of any potential conflicts. This disclosure is similar to the 408(b)(2) disclosure that retirement plan advisors must provide. While this law has been in effect since 2022, it's estimated that only 20% to 30% of employers have actually received these disclosures from their benefits brokers.

In the following sections, we will explore these two categories of compensation and examine why both direct and indirect payments can compromise a broker's ability to provide unbiased, objective advice, ultimately hindering employers from maximizing the return on their benefits investments.

Direct compensation

Many employers are aware that their broker receives commissions (typically 4% to 6% of the total premium) from health insurers, which means their income is directly tied to the cost of health insurance. However, in my experience, not all of them understand the clear conflict of interest this "direct" compensation creates. In the commission-based model, when costs go up, your broker's income also goes up. When costs go down, your broker's income also goes down. This directly contradicts the employer's goal of minimizing costs and maximizing value.

Since brokers' income is directly tied to the total premium paid by employers and employees, this system inherently discourages brokers from negotiating lower premiums or helping employers pursue more sophisticated financing and procurement strategies discussed later in this book. To help illustrate this dynamic, veteran HR professional Kate Shockey noted that brokers often say things like "What does your budgeted increase look like, or what are you expecting as an increase this year?"

Ironically, brokers who aggressively negotiate the best deals for employers often see their income suffer compared to those who simply maintain the status quo of annual renewal increases. This fundamental misalignment and the apathy resulting from it drive the $300 billion that employers overpay for on health insurance and healthcare each year.

Although some brokers have transitioned to fee-based compensation, many have not.

In a 2022 article from *Employee Benefit News*, Darren Fogarty observed, "Whereas the role of benefits brokers has shifted greatly, compensation models generally have not."[22] In other words, The benefits industry is still dominated by commissions. Gallagher's 2018 annual report, for instance, reveals a dependence on premium-based commissions.[23] It discloses that revenue may be "negatively impacted[ed]" by the "growing desire" of employer clients to pay them on a fee basis instead of commissions that "automatically increase." Gallagher's open admission and reluctance to financially align itself with employers—instead of insurers—is striking.

While benefits brokers generally mean well and provide a number of important services for employers, the financial conflict of interest created by their

22 D. Fogarty, "How to bring elevated standards, results and respect to the benefits industry", *Employee Benefit News* (12 October 2022), www.benefitnews.com/advisers/opinion/advisers-can-bring-new-standards-and-respect-to-the-benefits-industry, accessed June 15, 2025

23 A.J. Gallagher and Co., *2018 Annual Report: Expertise. Ethics. Excellence* (Arthur J. Gallagher and Co., 2019), https://s28.q4cdn.com/872121257/files/doc_financials/2018/ar/2018-Annual-Report.pdf, accessed June 15, 2025

commission-based revenue model has served brokers at the expense of employers and employees.

While commissions are the well-known primary revenue source for brokerage firms, the lesser-known MDI is a more critical concern. The CAA classifies MDI as "indirect compensation," and the MDI that insurers pay to brokers is highly detrimental, in that it largely exists to influence the recommendations brokers give to employers. Despite the requirement for this income to be listed on 408 disclosure forms, many employers of all sizes remain shockingly unaware of it.

Indirect compensation

In their 2018 earnings report, multinational brokerage firm Willis Towers Watson (WTW) defines MDI as "other revenue from insurance carriers" that takes "a variety of forms, including volume- or profit-based contingent commissions, facilities administration charges, business development agreements, and fees for providing certain data to carriers." This is a clear admission that their revenue stream extends beyond the commissions by insurers and fees paid by employers.

According to a 2005 article in KPMG's *Insurance Insider* publication, the late 1970s and early 1980s saw insurance brokers receiving money from both sides of the transaction: "As the fees were paid for a book of business encompassing numerous clients, it was difficult to determine the impact of individual clients. Therefore, there was little regulatory investigation into the practice."[24]

The article continues:

> "By the late 1980s, the practice had become widespread. At this point, many brokers were more focused on earning those contingent commissions than getting customers the best deal. But the arrangements were generally unknown outside the insurance industry."

The article gets right to the heart of the problem: who do benefits brokers serve? Employers? Health insurers? Or themselves?

By 2018, WTW acknowledged that "payments from carriers can incentivize intermediaries to put carriers' or their own interests ahead of their clients." This statement directly confirms the great misalignment at hand. When a broker prioritizes carrier relationships and revenue goals over the client's needs, it's the employer who ultimately suffers. WTW's report also notes that MDI may be subject to scrutiny by various regulators under conflict of interest, antitrust, unfair competition, conduct, and antibribery laws and

---

24 R. Wade, "A brief history of contingent commission agreements", *Insurance Journal* (January 24, 2005), www.insurancejournal.com/magazines/mag-features/2005/01/24/51209.htm, accessed June 15 2025

regulations. This highlights the potential for legal and ethical issues surrounding these types of payments.

Crucially, WTW also recognizes that "allegations of conflicts of interest, including in connection with accepting market-derived income... may have a material adverse effect on our business, financial condition, results of operation or reputation."

This suggests that even the brokers themselves acknowledge the potential harm their practices can cause.

There are various forms of MDI, and it's important for you to understand how each of them may impact the recommendations being made to you.

New business bonuses

Insurers use "New Business Bonuses" to encourage brokers to recommend their products. Since employers heavily depend on broker advice, these bonuses create a serious conflict of interest. Often labeled "churning" by regulators, these incentives can push brokers to switch employers to new plans, even when those plans don't align with their actual requirements or budget. While an initial offer from a new carrier might seem attractive due to artificial rate discounts, these discounts often vanish, resulting in steep price increases the following year. This strategy frequently drives up overall healthcare costs, damages employee morale, and leads to unnecessary change management.

Retention bonuses

Brokers aren't just rewarded for selling new plans. Retention bonuses reward brokers for keeping customers subscribed to their existing plans. This can create a perverse incentive that may ultimately harm employers by keeping them on suboptimal products. According to Mployer Advisor CEO Brian Freeman, "Brokers are often also paid contingent commissions from insurance carriers at the end of the year as bonuses for the number of clients placed with that carrier or for hitting retention numbers."[25]

These bonuses incentivize complacency and a lack of proactive exploration of better options. Brokers may be reluctant to recommend plan changes, even if those changes could significantly reduce costs or improve employee satisfaction, as it could jeopardize their retention bonus. This can result in employers being "locked in" to poor value, leading to higher premiums, limited network options, and, ultimately, increased healthcare costs for the employer and their

---

25 B. Freeman, "Understanding insurance brokers: The drivers of employee benefits costs", *Forbes* (August 11, 2023), www.forbes. com/councils/forbesbusinesscouncil/2023/08/11/understanding-insurance-brokers-the-drivers-of-employee-benefits-cost, accessed June 15, 2025

employees. An example of a retention bonus scheme is included below.

Insurer ABC's new "welcome back" bonus

Just in time for Q4, Insurer ABC introduced a new "welcome back" bonus when a group returns to Insurer ABC with a December 2020 or January 2021 effective date.

This is in addition to Insurer ABC's "Medical Incentive Program," which already offers $100 per member enrolling in qualifying products.

Program	Bonus paid
2021 new sales bonus	$6,000
2022 renewal bonus	$6,500
2023 renewal bonus	$7,000
Total bonus revenue per group	$19,500

Furthermore, retention bonuses discourage brokers from actively seeking out cost-saving opportunities for their clients. Instead of helping employers increase value by progressing through the Health Plan Maturity Model™ (discussed in later chapters), retention bonuses incentivize brokers to maintain the status quo of rising prices.

In short, retention bonuses create an environment in which brokers are rewarded for skimping on procurement, and this conflict ultimately undermines your ability to maximize the return on your organization's benefits investments.

Vacation gifts

For brokers who build exceptionally large books of business with an insurer, all-inclusive vacations are often offered as a "thank you" for being a good distribution partner. When I worked for a large insurer, I helped design bonus programs for our top-selling brokers and took them on all-inclusive vacations around the world. This was standard practice and no one gave it a second thought. Although these trips may seem innocuous, the allure of lavish vacations, fine-dining experiences, and other gifts can subconsciously, or even consciously, sway a broker's recommendations one way or another.

This subtle bias can lead to employers selecting plans with higher premiums, limited networks, or inadequate coverage, ultimately resulting in increased healthcare costs and decreased employee satisfaction. By prioritizing their own personal gain, even indirectly, brokers may be compromising your role as a fiduciary, for which you can be held personally responsible.

Payments from pharmacy benefit managers

A 2024 StatNews investigation revealed that "Consulting firms can collect at least $1 per prescription from the largest PBMs. This can go as high as $5 per prescription in extreme cases."[26] The relationship between insurers, brokers, and pharmacy benefit managers represents a hidden flow of money, often undisclosed to employers. This creates a significant conflict of interest, as these consultants are arguably working for PBMs, not employers.

David Smith further emphasizes this, saying, "They may bring in a pharmacy solution that is 'exclusive' to their clients, but they aren't telling their clients about the per-script fees or other revenue being generated through their arrangement."

Aon, Willis Towers Watson, Mercer, and Gallagher were cited in the article as major brokerage firms that collect per-script fees, and a lawsuit against Wells Fargo provided concrete examples of this conflict of interest in action. The complaint alleged that "Some employee benefits consultants (EBCs)… are in fact being paid by PBMs in ways that incentivize them to act against the plan's interests. For example, PBMs may promise to pay an EBC a commission on every prescription if the EBC recommends the PBM to its client plans."[27] This is a clear illustration of how kickbacks can influence recommendations.

---

26 B. Herman, "'It's beyond unethical': Opaque conflicts of interest permeate prescription drug benefits", *STAT* (June 20, 2023), www. statnews.com/2023/06/20/pbms-consulting-firms-investigation, accessed June 15, 2025

27 Navarro, Gamage, Bulla, and Kinsella v. Wells Fargo, United States District Court for the District of Minnesota, Civil Action No. 24-cv-3043

Loans and lines of credit

The financial entanglements go even deeper than PBM payments. Buried in the fine print of disclosures is a conflict arguably more powerful than any hidden fee: debt. In its own documents, industry giant Brown & Brown states it "may, on occasion, receive loans or credit from insurance companies."

With that single admission, the entire dynamic shifts to a creditor-debtor relationship that may significantly influence the recommendations being made to you by your broker.

In short, the ingrained practice of brokers accepting— and keeping—indirect payments from insurers and pharmacy benefit managers disqualifies them from serving you in a fiduciary capacity.

Such kickbacks from vendors directly undermine their ability to help you maximize your return on healthcare investments, leading to billions in healthcare overspend, reduced employee satisfaction, and a considerable reduction in your company's value.

Addressing the myth of large firm pricing power

There's a prevalent myth within the employee benefits industry that needs to be addressed. Insurers do not offer better pricing or terms to the clients of larger brokerage firms than small ones.

Despite this, big-box legacy brokerage firms like Aon, Mercer, Gallagher, and Brown & Brown sometimes convince employers that they secure better pricing or "deals" from health insurers due to the volume of business they place. For example, one national firm claims that, "Our size and scale ensure our clients get the most advanced and competitive programs. As a result, you will know you are accessing proven carriers with the industry's best terms, conditions, and pricing to support your employees while managing your budget." That size matters is a compelling narrative that might hold true in the property and casualty insurance sector, but it is categorically false in the employee benefits space.

The reality is that, despite what many employers have been led to believe, health insurers operate differently, and it's essential to understand that the system itself has perpetuated this myth, rather than any individual error or example of malpractice on the part of an employer. According to David Smith, SVP at Eben, "The idea that larger benefit firms can get better prices for their clients is as much a falsehood as the idea that a bunch of small businesses buying health insurance together will translate into cheaper rates." This isn't about blaming employers for not knowing better. The system itself is designed in a way that makes it difficult to see the truth.

In reality, health insurers maintain "the same quote on the street." This means that, if a soloist and the largest benefits firm in the world both request quotes from a carrier for the same employer (an event known as "dual activity" in the industry), the carrier will provide the same exact quote to both.

If large firms truly held pricing power, then the rampant consolidation we've seen throughout the brokerage industry would surely have driven health insurance rates down for employers. In reality, the opposite has taken place. The myth persists because it helps big-box legacy benefits firms win clients and keep employers locked into traditional, commission, and bonus-based models. It's important to understand that these practices are widespread in the industry, and many well-intentioned employers have fallen into these traps without realizing it.

CASE STUDY: Undisclosed compensation

The impact of misaligned commissions in the healthcare sector is best illustrated by recent litigation involving a top-three benefits broker who, unfortunately, will need to remain nameless for the purposes of the book. They were contracted to provide employee benefits consulting services to a large government employer from 2012 to 2019. Being a self-funded plan, the client's aim was to have its broker improve the value of the program by managing its healthcare supply chain and procuring the best administrator, network, pharmacy benefits manager (PBM), and reinsurance for the organization.

They needed a benefits consultant to act "in the best interest of its employees."

The relationship broke down and ended up in a well-publicized legal case. The client accused the unnamed broker of breaching its agreements and trust by receiving "secret insurance commissions over the years totaling millions of dollars from insurance carriers." The following direct quote does a great job of paraphrasing the case: "The client had engaged a consultant getting paid more from the carriers it was to scrutinize and supervise than from the client itself."

The client claimed the broker failed to disclose these commissions, despite representations that "We will fully disclose all compensation received" and that "We will represent your best interests in all ongoing interactions with carriers and vendors."

The client accused the broker of breach of contract, breach of fiduciary duty, fraud in the inducement, and fraudulent concealment. Furthermore, they alleged the brokers' actions were motivated by "greed."

The client sought damages, including the disgorgement of the secret commissions, and requested that all recovered damages be contributed to a trust to benefit their employees. In response, predictably, the broker filed a motion to dismiss the lawsuit, stating, "Apparently, the client believes attaching the description 'secret' to commissions somehow makes the commissions nefarious," and did not feel the need to admit to any wrongdoing.

However, they eventually decided to settle rather than risk going to court, and, ultimately, the client pocketed over $500,000 in the settlement. The two parties reached an agreement under which the broker did not have to admit to any wrongdoing, and both parties declined to comment further on the settlement. This prompted my decision to keep everyone anonymous in this case study; however, with a bit of research, you should be able to find details of the widely reported case.

Before uncovering the alleged conflicts, the client, like many large employers, felt trapped in a cycle of rising healthcare costs and stagnant benefits. They believed they were receiving expert, objective guidance from a large benefits broker. However, a growing unease lingered, a suspicion that their interests were not fully aligned with those advising them. This unease was validated when they discovered the undisclosed commissions.

This pivotal moment served as a catalyst for radical change. The client, determined to break free from the constraints of conflicted counsel, took decisive action. They fired both their broker and insurer, effectively dismantling the system that had kept them in the dark. This bold move was the first step towards securing the unbiased advice they desperately needed.

With a clean slate, the employer embarked on a comprehensive overhaul of its benefits program. Freed from the influence of hidden financial ties, they gained access to a world of innovative solutions and cost-saving opportunities that had previously been obscured.

They leveraged their size to negotiate directly with providers, eliminating unnecessary intermediaries and implementing innovative cost-containment strategies. This newfound transparency and control enabled them to tailor their benefits program to the specific needs of their employee population, resulting in significant improvements in both cost and quality.

In the context of the Health Plan Maturity Model (HPMM) discussed later in this book, they moved from a "growth" stage using traditional vendors in an "administrative services only" (ASO) capacity for their self-funded plan, skipped the "enterprise" stage, and went directly to the "exit" stage with direct contracts, steerage, and advanced procurement methods.

The results were astounding. By securing unbiased advice and taking ownership of their benefits strategy, the employer saved an estimated $40 million over the next few years. This remarkable turnaround not only improved their financial health but also demonstrated the profound impact of transparency and accountability in the healthcare industry. This employer's experience underscores the importance of seeking truly unbiased advice, a crucial step in unlocking the potential for significant improvements in employee benefits. For their innovative approach to healthcare benefits, the employer was recognized with local industry awards.

Key takeaways

- The brokerage industry was created by insurers to sell their products.

- Brokers get paid by insurers and make more money when your costs go up—not down.

- Large brokerage firms get the same pricing and terms from health insurers as small firms and solo agents.

Action items

- Consider the impact of conflicted advice on your company's healthcare spending.

- Question the reasoning behind your broker's recommendations and consider getting a second opinion.

- Ask your broker to complete an ERISA 408(b)(2) (B) compensation disclosure. This is required by law so that you know who pays them—and how much. Be sure to look at the section on "indirect compensation," so that you know how their recommendations may be biased.

You can download a 408 disclosure template by scanning the QR code below, or visiting www.fixinghealthcare.com/disclosure

FOUR

The Solution
Fiduciary Thinking And Unbiased Advice

A s an executive, you are likely a fiduciary of your company's health and welfare plans.

Under federal law, this means you have a legal and ethical obligation to act in the best interests of plan participants. This responsibility requires moving beyond simply accepting the status quo and actively seeking unbiased advice and transparency from vendors.

Moving beyond the status quo: Embracing your fiduciary role

The status quo in healthcare benefits is unsustainable. Continuing to accept ever-increasing prices, opaque contracts, and conflicted advice is not only fiscally irresponsible; it will damage your reputation and, due to the nature of your responsibilities as a fiduciary, pose a significant legal risk for which you can be held personally liable. Equally important, perpetuating the status quo represents a catastrophic missed opportunity for genuine economic growth, a stronger workforce, and more prosperous communities.

NOTE

The federal government's Employee Retirement Income Security Act (ERISA) of 1974 establishes fiduciary responsibilities and standards for those who manage plan assets... Yes, that's probably you.

In what follows, we will begin to explore the solutions to this problem and delve into the concept of fiduciary duty, and why unbiased advice is non-negotiable. In later chapters, I will introduce the Total Benefits Assessment™, Health Plan Maturity Model™, and APIM™ (Assess, Procure, Implement, Manage) frameworks, which serve as blueprints for continuous benefits optimization. This combination of tools and methodologies will transform your health plans from cost centers into strategic assets that increase cash flow, productivity, and the value of your organization.

Understanding fiduciary duty in healthcare benefits

A fundamental principle underpins true healthcare reform: the fiduciary advantage. In this paradigm shift, we move beyond relational transactions based on blind trust, to partnerships based on radical transparency, alignment, and legal obligation.

The advantage is that, unlike many compliance requirements in employee benefits, which often serve merely as compliance exercises, applying fiduciary standards and practices adds genuine value to your organization.

But who is a fiduciary, and what does it mean to be one? To provide you with the most accurate information possible, I am going to quote, paraphrase, and summarize a fantastic resource that was developed by the Department of Labor's (DOL) Employee Benefits Security Administration (EBSA) entitled Understanding Your Fiduciary Responsibilities Under A Group Health Plan.

To access the DOL's original document, visit www.dol.gov/node/63394 or scan the QR code below:

Let's begin.

Who is a fiduciary?

According to the Department of Labor, "A person using discretion in administering and managing a plan or controlling the plan's assets is a fiduciary to the extent of that discretion or control. Thus, fiduciary status is based on the functions performed for the plan, not just a person's title."

That being said, there's a good chance that you are a fiduciary. If so, keep reading…

Defining fiduciary duty

In plain terms, "fiduciary duty" means that you are legally and ethically bound to manage your employees' health plans with absolute care and loyalty. You are obligated to act *solely* in the best interests of your plan participants and their families. You're entrusted with their financial well-being and their healthcare needs. Period. You're not just managing a program; you're helping to safeguard people's lives and livelihoods.

Key responsibilities of a fiduciary

Fiduciaries in employer-sponsored health plans have several critical responsibilities:

- **Acting in the best interests of plan participants:** The main responsibility of a fiduciary is to act exclusively in the best interests of plan participants and beneficiaries. This entails making decisions that prioritize their well-being and financial security, even if those decisions may not provide direct benefits to the employer.

- **Exercising prudence:** Fiduciaries must act with the care, skill, prudence, and diligence that a knowledgeable and reasonable person would exercise in similar situations. This includes performing thorough research, obtaining expert advice when necessary, and documenting the decision-making process. As the DOL notes, "Prudence focuses on the process for making fiduciary decisions, so a fiduciary should document decisions and the basis for those decisions." Note: In a later chapter, I'll provide some guidance and criteria for identifying "expert advice."

- **Following plan documents:** Fiduciaries must follow the governing plan documents of the health plan. This includes adhering to the plan's terms, conditions, and procedures concerning administration, eligibility, and claims processing. The DOL emphasizes, "Following the terms of the plan document is also an important responsibility. The plan document serves as the foundation for plan operations." Note: Although most companies hire a plan administrator (aka:

"Third-Party Administrator" (TPA)) to execute their plan document and process claims, it is ultimately your responsibility as a fiduciary to make sure the document is being followed.

- **Paying only reasonable plan expenses:** As a fiduciary, you must ensure that all fees and expenses charged to plan assets are reasonable and necessary for the operation of the plan. The DOL states, "While the law does not specify a permissible level of fees, it does require that fees charged to a plan be 'reasonable.'"

Legal ramifications of breaching fiduciary duty

The legal consequences of breaching fiduciary duty can be severe, and fiduciaries who fail to meet their obligations may be held personally liable for any losses resulting from a breach. These ramifications include:

- **Financial penalties:** Fiduciaries may be required to restore any losses to the plan, as well as any profits they made through improper use of plan assets.

- **Lawsuits:** Plan participants and beneficiaries can bring lawsuits against fiduciaries for breaches of duty, seeking monetary damages and other legal remedies.

- **Reputational damage:** Breaching fiduciary duty can severely damage an employer's reputation, resulting in decreased employee morale, difficulty attracting top talent, and negative publicity.

The Department of Labor explicitly states that "Fiduciaries who don't follow the basic standards of conduct may be personally liable to restore any losses to the plan, or to restore any profits made through improper use of the plan's assets resulting from their actions." In simpler terms, if you fail to manage your benefits programs with diligence and prudence, you could be held personally accountable for breaches of fiduciary duty.

Cultivating a fiduciary mindset: Practical steps

To ensure you are fulfilling your fiduciary duties, consider the following:

- Ask your current broker for a full disclosure of all compensation, both direct and indirect, as mandated by the Consolidated Appropriations Act (CAA).

- Implement a checklist for plan reviews. Regularly review your plan documents, vendor contracts, and claims data. Document your decision-making process.

- Seek independent, unbiased advice. Consider engaging a fiduciary-based management consulting firm, or bring benefits expertise in-house... More on this later.

- Educate yourself and your team on fiduciary responsibilities and best practices.

- Demand transparency from all vendors. Request detailed reports on costs, rebates, and utilization.

In recent years, the number of lawsuits against fiduciaries has increased. High-profile lawsuits against major corporations, such as Wells Fargo, Johnson & Johnson, and JP Morgan Chase, serve as sobering reminders that this liability is a tangible and growing risk. Therefore, understanding and fully embracing your fiduciary role is not just a matter of compliance but also about safeguarding your organization and its employees. It's about moving beyond surface-level management to genuine stewardship.

Unbiased advice

I have written at length about the conflict of interest inherent in broker relationships, but it's worth taking a pause to reflect on the current situation. As an executive, would you ever work with a CPA who got paid by the IRS? What if the IRS paid that CPA a commission based on a percentage of the taxes collected from your business? Of course not. No one would accept these terms because the CPA's advice would always be skewed and you'd end up paying more in taxes than you should.

It might seem obvious when we put it in those terms, but in reality, that is how much of the U.S. benefits industry works today. As ludicrous as it sounds, the revenue model of the benefits brokerage industry is metaphorically the same as working with a CPA who gets paid by the IRS. In this setup, employers are likely to pay more for healthcare than necessary because benefits brokers, who are supposed to negotiate pricing and terms with insurers on behalf of employers and their employees, actually earn more when healthcare costs go up rather than down.

To avoid this dynamic, employers have two options:

1. Bring benefits expertise in-house.

2. Partner with management consulting firms that serve as fiduciaries to you and specialize in employee benefits financing, procurement, and management.

Bringing benefits expertise in-house

In the spring of 2016, famed entrepreneur Mark Cuban founded his latest venture, Cost Plus Drugs. This initiative sought to disrupt the prescription drug industry, which Cuban believed was marred by opacity and exorbitant costs. While Cuban had embraced disruption throughout his business career, he admitted that, like many CEOs, he had never fully scrutinized his company's health plan for potential improvements.

During an interview on the "Relentless Health Value" podcast, he expressed that, "as CEO, the last thing you feel like doing is sitting through a meeting to go over the details of your insurance policies."[28] However, when Cuban decided to go over those details, he was shocked to discover that his sickest employees were inadvertently funding pharmacy rebates returned to his company. This revelation served as one of the catalysts for founding the Mark Cuban Cost Plus Drug Company—a direct-to-consumer pharmacy dedicated to radical transparency and fair pricing.

As Cuban delved deeper into the intricacies of what had turned into a significant expense for his companies, he unearthed layers of conflict and waste. When discussing his former broker at a Texas Hall of Fame event in March of 2025, Cuban explained:

---

28 M. Cuban, "Episode 418: Mark Cuban with some advice for CEOs and CFOs of self-insured employers", Relentless Health Value (2023), https://relentlesshealthvalue.com/episode/ep418-mark-cuban-with-some-advice-for-ceos-and-cfos-of-self-insured-employers-with-mark-cuban-and-ferrin-williams-pharmd-mba-from-scripta, accessed June 15, 2025

"I used to use my guy, who was a world-class consultant, right? My guy would come in every year when we're looking at our new plans, and say, 'Look, their price is going up 7%, but I'm taking care of you. You're only going up four percent.' When we started Cost Plus Drugs, I started understanding the industry more, and I looked at the details of what my guy was offering me. For example, I looked at generic drug spending at the Mavs over an 18-month period, and we were charged $169,000. The price with Cost Plus was $19,000. Needless to say, he's not my guy anymore. And that's a challenge for CEOs right now."[29]

Since learning about the conflicts of interest within the brokerage and healthcare industry, Cuban—like myself and many others—has become radicalized.

For companies that do not have existing Total Rewards or Benefits leaders, Cuban has been encouraging corporations to go as far as creating a new "Chief Benefits Officer" (CBO) role. This is for good reason.

Many corporations, typically larger ones, recognize the substantial financial implications of employee healthcare and have invested in in-house benefits

29 W. Maddox, "Mark Cuban: CEOs should create a new C-suite role", *D Magazine* (March 11, 2025), www.dmagazine.com/healthcare-business/2025/03/mark-cuban-ceos-should-create-a-new-c-suite-role, accessed June 15, 2025

expertise. This approach aims to provide direct control over the financing, procurement, and management of healthcare for their employees, ensuring alignment with the company's strategic objectives. By hiring dedicated benefits professionals directly, these companies seek to minimize the conflicts of interest that arise from relying solely on the advice of external brokerage firms. Internal experts can deliver unbiased advice, rooted in a deep understanding of the company's workforce and financial goals, ultimately tailoring benefits programs to maximize effectiveness and cost efficiency.

Think of it this way: just as a large company wouldn't outsource its entire finance department or rely solely on external lawyers for all legal matters, many are realizing that healthcare benefits deserve the same level of dedicated in-house attention. Companies routinely bring finance, legal services, and tax compliance in-house because these areas are critical to their financial health and strategic direction. The move towards hiring in-house benefits expertise aligns with the same principles. It's about recognizing that employee healthcare is not just an expense but a crucial investment in the workforce and a key component of the company's overall strategy.

Of course, companies that have in-house benefits expertise may use external benefits firms for more mundane, low-value transactional tasks. In this case, your Chief Benefits Officer is free to focus on the

high-value activities within benefits consulting, procurement, and overall program management that I'll
describe in a later section of the book.

This shift in-house is a fundamental change in approach.
Companies are realizing that building a robust internal benefits team is an investment in their future—a
strategic move that empowers them to navigate the
complexities of healthcare with confidence and clarity. Imagine a world in which employers are not just
passive consumers of pre-packaged plans, but active
architects of their own benefits ecosystems. This is the
promise of in-house expertise: a future where healthcare is not a burden but a powerful tool for attracting
talent, fostering a healthy workforce, and driving sustainable growth. It represents a journey towards greater
control, transparency, and ultimately, a healthier, more
prosperous future for all.

While the initial investment in hiring a Chief Benefits
Officer (CBO) may appear substantial, the potential
return on investment can be significant.

A skilled CBO can actively manage healthcare costs,
negotiate better vendor contracts, and implement
data-driven strategies to generate substantial savings.
For example, compared to sticking with traditional
broker recommendations, a company with 1,000
employees enrolled in its health plan could save any-
where from $1,000 to $3,000 per employee per year
with a CBO. This shift could represent annual savings

of between $1 million to $3 million for the company. With a CBO's salary of approximately $300,000, the potential return on investment for the company could range from a conservative 3:1 at the low end to 10:1 at the top end. Additionally, before hiring the CBO, the company is likely to remove high-value services from its benefits firm's scope, allowing it to negotiate lower commissions and fees from them. This can lead to a rapid recovery of the CBO's salary and benefits, resulting in long-term financial gains for the company, improved employee satisfaction, and other reduced administrative burdens.

For businesses that do not have the size needed to justify bringing benefits expertise in-house, replacing legacy brokers with the new breed of fiduciary-based management consulting firms represents a tremendous opportunity to improve the financial and physical health of organizations.

Fiduciary-based management consulting firms

In an earlier chapter, I shared my personal experience of being fired from a large brokerage firm for advocating on behalf of my clients. This experience led me to found Health Compass Consulting, one of the first fiduciary-based management consulting firms that prioritizes unbiased advice, transparency, and financial alignment over everything else.

With Health Compass's liberated and financially independent business model, I was able to save my first client $3,026 per employee while improving network access and coverage. This was an economic empowerment strategy that left the company in a better position to exit, which they did, at a nice multiple, the following year.

This one example illustrates the power of unbiased advice and strategic healthcare management. When employers are freed from the constraints of the traditional brokerage model, they can make decisions that truly benefit their employees and their bottom line. They can unlock financial flexibility, fuel economic growth, and provide employees with the stability they need to pursue their goals and live inspired lives.

As an employer, you are a fiduciary of your employee benefits plan, and ERISA requires fiduciaries who lack technical expertise in the benefits space to hire certified professionals. Certified experts who work at fiduciary-based benefits firms fill this role. Additionally, ERISA also requires employers to hire benefits firms that are unconflicted for consulting and procurement services. Since fiduciary-based firms do not accept compensation from health insurers, PBMs, or associated vendors (with some exceptions outlined by the Validation Institute), they are uniquely positioned to help employers fill this critical role.

Remember that Willis Towers Watson, worth $33.62 billion, explicitly stated the following in their 2018 financial report: "Payments from carriers can incentivize intermediaries to put carriers' or their own interests ahead of their clients." This is a direct admission of the conflict of interest inherent in the legacy brokerage model, and evidence that a new way of working is long overdue.

Luckily for employers, a new breed of management consulting firms has been emerging in the market since 2016 or so. Like me, many of their founders came from various parts of the benefits industry, saw the misalignment, and sought better ways to help businesses achieve their objectives. Many of them were also inspired by Health Rosetta founder Dave Chase's 2017 book *CEOs Guide to Restoring the American Dream: How to deliver world class healthcare to your employees at half the cost.*[30] This book, along with Chase's Health Rosetta organization, challenged the old ways of doing things and inspired hundreds of benefits professionals to adopt fiduciary-based thinking to better serve employers.

Unlike brokers who get paid to sell products for insurers, fiduciary-based management consultants get paid by employers to provide a combination of benefits

---

30   D. Chase, *CEO's Guide to Restoring the American Dream: How to deliver world class healthcare to your employees at half the cost* (Health Rosetta Media, 2017)

consulting, procurement, implementation, and management services. Since they do not accept compensation from vendors, they are unconflicted and can thereby serve as a fiduciary to you.

When you partner with a fiduciary advisor, you gain the assurance that their recommendations are rooted solely in your best interests. They are not influenced by commissions, bonuses, or other financial incentives from insurance carriers or vendors. This allows for a truly objective, data-driven approach to benefits management. In my experience, shifting to a fee-based model that eliminates commissions and kickbacks has been transformative. At a stroke, it creates the freedom to analyze a wider range of health insurance products and custom solutions without any external pressure. It allows for the development of contracts that ensure 100% of any vendor bonuses are returned to the client, further solidifying the commitment to financial alignment.

This model ensures that the focus remains squarely on maximizing the return on your benefits investment. There is no incentive to push one product over another or to prioritize the premiums that generate larger commissions. The sole objective is to deliver value, optimize outcomes, and ensure that your benefits program serves the best interests of your organization and your employees.

I created the following table to illustrate the differences between brokers and fiduciary-based firms:

Feature	Legacy brokers	Fiduciary firms
Compensation	Primarily commission based, tied to sales of insurance products. May include bonuses and other indirect compensation from insurers.	Fee based, agreed upon with the client. No commissions or bonuses from health insurers.
Incentives	Incentivized to sell products that generate higher commissions. May prioritize insurer relationships.	Incentivized to act solely in the client's best interest.
Obligations	Acts as a sales agent for the insurer. No legal obligation to put the client's interests above their own.	Legally bound to act as a fiduciary, prioritizing the client's interests.
Transparency	Disclosure of compensation may be limited or unclear.	Full transparency of fees and potential conflicts of interest.

The limitations of the legacy brokerage model vs. fiduciary advice

Fiduciary-based firms do not work in isolation. They work within the existing marketplace, so it is essential to understand how they handle indirect compensation and situations where commissions cannot be removed. This is a critical aspect of ensuring transparency and maintaining the unconflicted nature of the relationship. These best practices are similar to those adopted by the 401(k) industry when fiduciary standards started being applied in the early 2000s, where hidden fees and kickbacks were eliminated to protect plan participants.

There are two practices that are crucial for maintaining the integrity of the fiduciary relationship and ensuring that the employer's interests are always prioritized. By mirroring the successful transitions of the retirement industry, we can build trust and confidence in these practices within the health and welfare sector:

- **Crediting back bonuses and indirect compensation:** A firm's contract with employers should explicitly state that the firm credits 100% of any bonus or form of indirect compensation received from vendors back to the employer. This ensures that any financial incentives from vendors are passed directly to the employer, further solidifying the firm's role as an unconflicted advocate.

- **Commissions that cannot be removed:** In some rare situations, commissions cannot be removed from certain insurance products. In such cases, the fiduciary-based firm will credit those commissions towards its fee. This means that the employer is not paying a commission within the premium as well as a separate fee to the firm. The commission simply reduces the overall fee charged by the firm.

The importance of adhering to fiduciary standards has been brought into sharp focus in the past year with a flurry of lawsuits aimed at major employers like Johnson & Johnson, Wells Fargo, and JP Morgan. In these suits, employees allege that plan fiduciaries (CFOs, board members, etc) failed to fulfill their fiduciary responsibilities under ERISA. Notably, these lawsuits have also named the employers' benefits firms (ie, brokers) and PBMs, highlighting the interconnected nature of fiduciary responsibility in the benefits ecosystem. These legal challenges serve as a stark reminder of the potential consequences of failing to properly manage and oversee employee benefits plans.

NOTE

In many states, the compensation built into small group (less than fifty employees) fully insured health plans cannot be removed. This is an example of where the benefits firm should credit this compensation toward their annual or monthly fee.

Compensating fiduciary-based firms: Dispelling pricing myths

One of the biggest misconceptions about fiduciary-based firms is how they are compensated. Many employers believe that hiring a management consulting firm will cost them an additional large sum of money, and in many cases, this is false. Since fiduciary-based firms remove all commissions from health insurance products during the procurement process, their fee may be lower, equal to, or higher than the commissions paid to your broker.

Here's a breakdown:

- **Removing commissions:** During the procurement for health plans, fiduciary-based firms instruct insurers to remove all commissions from the health plans, and this request is commonplace. This means that the employer is no longer paying the commissions that are usually embedded in their premiums.

- **Fee-based compensation:** Instead of commissions, these firms charge a fee for their consulting, procurement, and management services. This fee is transparent and agreed upon with you in advance.

Having turned their backs on commissions and bonuses, fiduciary-based firms use various pricing methodologies to be compensated for their work.

These include:

- **Per employee per month (PEPM):** A fee is charged for each employee enrolled in the health plan.

- **Flat monthly or annual fee:** A fixed fee is charged for the services provided.

- **Flat fee plus performance-based compensation:** A base fee is charged, with additional compensation based on achieving specific savings targets.

- **Performance-based considerations:** Performance-based compensation is a great tool for aligning incentives with outcomes, but it comes with a warning. Employers must have full visibility and understanding of how "savings" are defined in advance of any commitment. Is it against the expected increase, last year's spend, or another benchmark? It's also important to understand that, if too much of the firm's compensation is based on a percentage of savings, the firm may intentionally or unintentionally push its client through the Health Plan Maturity Model (discussed in the next chapter) at an accelerated pace to maximize savings. Discounting the employer's bandwidth, perceptions of risk, and tolerance for change management may lead to a poor client experience. To mitigate this, I recommend that performance-based compensation not exceed 25% of savings and that savings be clearly defined and measured over a reasonable timeframe, to account for the natural fluctuations in claims.

CASE STUDY: The power of fiduciary guidance

The following case study exemplifies how a fiduciary-based management consulting firm helped an employer move beyond traditional healthcare approaches to achieve significant cost savings and improved employee benefits. This story underscores the core thesis of this book: that executives who seek out unbiased expert advice can take control of their healthcare spending and achieve optimal outcomes.

E-Powered Benefits is a pioneering fiduciary-based benefits firm on the West Coast founded by the aforementioned David Contorno and led by Emma Fox. This case study tracks an employer's medical and pharmacy costs and plan enrollment over a three-year period, during which their employee count grew from 435 to over 700. This growth alone typically leads to increased healthcare costs, but this employer bucked that trend by partnering with E-Powered Benefits and implementing their independent strategic benefits model.

E-Powered Benefits designed and implemented a model that incorporated several key components, all aimed at transparency, cost control, and quality care:

- **An independent third-party administrator (TPA):** Using a TPA with 14,000 direct contracts provided greater flexibility and control over plan design and administration, facilitated by E-Powered Benefits.

- **A transparent PBM:** E-Powered Benefits secured a PBM that actively assisted with drugs covered under Patient Assistance Programs or imported internationally, ensuring cost-effective access to medications.

- **Clinically based medical management:** E-Powered Benefits implemented proper, clinically driven medical management to ensure that care was appropriate and necessary, reducing wasteful spending.

- **Reference-based pricing:** E-Powered Benefits implemented this strategy, which tied reimbursement rates to actual costs, eliminating inflated charges and promoting fairness in pricing.

Although some organizations have an aversion to Reference-Based Pricing (RBP), E-Powered Benefits methodically assessed the employer to see if the pricing strategy supported the employer's objectives. It did, and so was implemented to much success.

To analyze the impact of E-Powered Benefits' approach, the employer's total medical and pharmacy costs were tracked and divided by the sum of each month's members covered (member months) for each year. These per member per month (PMPM) costs were then compared to the Kaiser Family Foundation's Employer Healthcare Benefit Survey single premium for the same year. The Kaiser Family Foundation costs were reduced by 20% to estimate medical and pharmacy costs only and exclude overhead or fixed costs. This adjustment makes the benchmark comparable to E-Powered Benefits' costs.

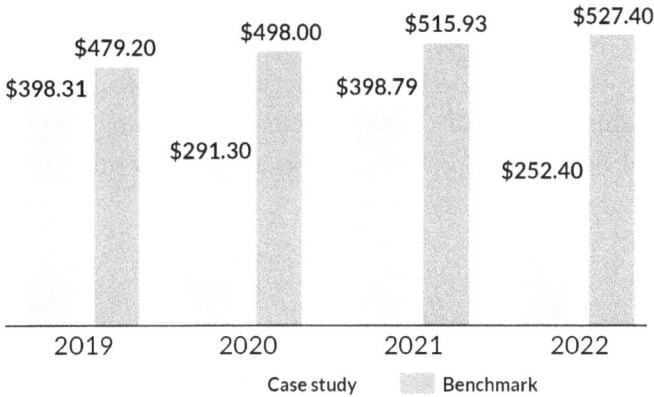

The chart above shows the case study's per member per month costs for 2019 through 2022 plan years along with the benchmark adjusted to reflect only medical and pharmacy costs.

The benchmark was from 20% to 109% higher than the costs achieved by E-Powered Benefits.

This case study demonstrates the power of moving beyond traditional healthcare models with the guidance and expertise of a firm like E-Powered Benefits. By embracing transparency, independent administration, and clinically driven care management, E-Powered Benefits helped this employer achieve significant cost reductions against industry standard costs, while still providing quality benefits to their growing workforce. This success is a testament to the principles outlined in this book and the potential for businesses to take control of their healthcare spending when they partner with knowledgeable and innovative firms. It highlights that, by progressing through the Health Plan Maturity Model with highly seasoned support, businesses can achieve not only cost savings but also a healthier and more engaged workforce.

Key takeaways

- Executives are often fiduciaries of their company's health and welfare plans.

- Fiduciaries have a legal and ethical obligation to act in the best interests of plan participants.

- Unbiased advice and transparency are essential for effective benefits management.

- Fiduciaries can be held personally liable for breaching fiduciary standards.

Action items

- Share this book and DOL guidelines with members of your team.

- If you don't have a separate fiduciary committee for health and welfare plans (not retirement plans), work with benefits professionals to create one.

FIVE

Success Tools, Models, And Frameworks

W e've established the critical need for change in how businesses manage their healthcare benefits provisions. We've discussed the fiduciary imperative of unbiased advice and the broader economic empowerment that can be achieved through strategic benefits management. Now, let's dive into some practical steps that will help you through the required transformation. The first of these is the APIM Framework.

The APIM Framework: Building your ideal benefits program

Whether you're using in-house resources or an external fiduciary-based firm, having an overall annual process for managing and optimizing your benefits program is essential for success. After years of trial and error, we developed the APIM Framework as a way of categorizing and managing the services needed to maximize healthcare investments.

Assess Procure
Implement Manage™
From Health Compass Consulting

The architect (Assess)

If you're building a home, you would initially hire an architect. After assessing your needs, values, and vision, the architect designs a blueprint. Since every organization has its own needs and standard of value, having a formal process for understanding these dynamics is essential for long-term success.

In the APIM Framework, the "Assess" stage is like the architect's work. A service-based benefits firm acts as your architect, conducting a thorough Total Benefits Assessment™ (TBA), as discussed later in this chapter. They collect data, analyze your current program, identify needs, and create a strategic plan tailored to your organization. As with an architect, they don't just sell you a pre-made plan; they design a custom solution based on sound, independent professional judgement.

The general contractor (Procure and Implement)

Next, you'd hire a general contractor. The general contractor takes the architect's blueprints and brings them to life. They procure the best subcontractors, negotiate contracts, manage the construction process, and ensure everything is built according to plan.

Management consulting firms act as your general contractor, helping you select the right vendors, negotiate contracts, design your plan, and manage the implementation process. They ensure a smooth transition and effective communication with your employees. They build the structure of your benefits program.

The property manager (Manage)

Finally, once the house is built, you might hire a property manager to handle ongoing maintenance, address issues, and ensure the house remains in good condition. They provide ongoing support and ensure your investment is protected.

In the APIM Framework, the "Manage" stage is like the property manager's work. The service-based benefits firm acts as your property manager, continuously monitoring your program, tracking performance, making adjustments, and ensuring ongoing compliance. They provide ongoing support and ensure your benefits program continues to deliver value. They maintain and optimize the structure of your benefits program.

The APIM Framework is a systematic approach to optimizing your employee health benefits program. It's designed to move you from reactive management to proactive, strategic control. It's not about applying quick fixes or band-aids, but is about building a solid foundation for long-term success, just like building a house.

The framework is based on the understanding that effective benefits management is an ongoing process, not a one-time event. It requires continuous assessment, strategic procurement, seamless implementation, and diligent management. By following the APIM Framework, you can ensure that your benefits program is aligned with your business goals, meets the needs of your employees, and delivers maximum value, just like a well-built and well-maintained house.

Now I've shared some definitions, let's look into the four phases of activity in more depth, remembering our house-building analogy.

1. Assess (the architect)

This is where the journey begins. As discussed, TBA is a critical tool in this phase. But the "Assess" stage goes beyond the TBA to create a detailed plan akin to an architect's drawings. It involves:

- **Data collection:** Gathering all relevant information about your current benefits program, like surveying the land and existing structures.

- **Analysis:** Examining the data to identify trends, patterns, and areas of concern, like analyzing the soil and existing utilities.

- **Benchmarking:** Comparing your program's performance to industry standards and best practices, like comparing your design to other successful builds.

- **Interviews:** Surveying decision makers to better understand their goals, perceptions of risk, tolerance to change management, and understanding of healthcare financing and procurement.

- **Identifying opportunities:** Pinpointing areas where you can save money, enhance benefits, improve efficiency, and reduce risk, like identifying potential improvements and cost savings in the blueprint.

- **Strategic planning:** After your data has been collected and analyzed, your team will meet with you to create goals and develop the roadmaps needed to achieve them.

2. Procure (the general contractor—part 1)

Once you have a clear understanding of your current state and your goals, it's time to "Procure" the right solutions.

This involves:

- **Defining requirements:** Based on the assessment, you define your specific needs and requirements for vendors and solutions, like outlining the materials and specifications for the build.

- **Vendor selection:** Researching and evaluating potential vendors, like selecting reliable subcontractors.

- **Negotiation:** Negotiating contracts and terms with selected vendors, like negotiating prices and timelines with subcontractors.

NOTE

There's a good chance that you have never been shown even a fraction of the ways healthcare can be financed and procured for your organization. That being said, many executives find a comprehensive procurement process highly enlightening and encouraging

---

3. Implement (the general contractor—part 2)

With the right solutions in place, it's time to "Implement" them effectively.

Continuing with our analogy, this involves:

- **Communication:** Clearly communicating changes and updates to employees, like keeping the homeowner informed of progress.

- **Enrollment:** Facilitating a smooth enrollment process, like managing inspections and approvals.

- **Transition:** Managing the transition from the old program to the new program, like handing over the keys to the new house.

- **Training:** Providing training to HR staff and employees on new processes and systems, like providing instructions on how to use new appliances.

4. Manage (the property manager)

The process doesn't end with implementation. Effective benefits management is an ongoing endeavor.

As a result, the "Manage" stage involves:

- **Monitoring:** Continuously monitoring the performance of your benefits program, like regular maintenance and inspections.

- **Reporting:** Generating regular reports to track progress and identify areas for improvement, like providing updates to the homeowner.

- **Optimization:** Making adjustments and refinements to your program based on data and feedback, like making repairs and upgrades as needed.

- **Compliance:** Ensuring ongoing compliance with regulations and requirements, like ensuring the house meets building codes.

The APIM Framework is a continuous cycle, just like maintaining a house, which requires ongoing attention. The "Manage" stage often leads back to the "Assess" stage, as you identify new opportunities for improvement and begin the process again.

The Total Benefits Assessment™ (TBA)

While delivering a consulting project to a large hospice group that was acquiring another company in the winter of 2024, the acquiring company's CEO butted in to ask their HR Director, "Is our benefits program getting better, or worse?" This seemingly simple question had the HR Director scrambling for an answer. Answering it was difficult because the value equation of a benefits program is complex, and no one had ever helped them quantify it. After all, what does "better" mean, and to whom?

Although the proposition of quantifying the value equation of a benefits program had been rolling around in my head for some time, this conversation was a turning point. We needed a more comprehensive approach to quantifying the performance of a benefits program so that we could more easily help our clients identify opportunities, set goals, develop roadmaps, and measure progress over time. This realization led to the development of the Total Benefits Assessment™ (TBA), our proprietary measurement methodology, which has become central to our work at Health Compass Consulting.

The TBA is our framework for continuous improvement, guiding our entire customer journey. It's a diagnostic tool that helps us benchmark an organization's current state, identify gaps and opportunities, and track progress over time. It answers the tricky director's question: "Is our benefits program better or worse?" And more importantly, it challenges them, too, by asking, "How can we make it better?"

It's important to note that while the TBA is a unique methodology developed through our experience and insights, there are certainly other frameworks and approaches in the market that organizations can use to assess and improve their benefits programs. My goal is to share our particular approach, which we have found to be highly effective, and offer it as a valuable tool for your consideration. Whatever tools you adopt, the important thing is to measure your performance objectively.

Measurement becomes important in today's complex healthcare landscape because managing employee benefits is more than just a transactional task, it's a strategic imperative. A well-designed benefits program can attract and retain top talent, boost employee morale and productivity, and improve overall organizational health. Conversely, a poorly managed program can lead to wasted spending, compliance risks, and disengaged employees. Where do you lie between these two benchmarks? It's hard to tell if you don't investigate.

The initial version of the TBA consists of just twenty-five questions, takes about five minutes to complete, and doesn't require any data collection by you. Once complete, you'll be able to review your results and compare your scores to the hundreds of other companies that have taken it.

The TBA is important because it allows you to:

- **Quantify your value equation:** Understand the true return on your benefits investment.

- **Benchmark your performance:** See how your program compares to industry standards and best practices.

- **Identify opportunities for improvement:** Uncover areas where you can save money, enhance benefits, and improve efficiency.

- **Track progress over time:** Monitor the impact of changes and measure the success of your strategies.

- **Make data-driven decisions:** Move beyond guesswork and rely on solid evidence to guide your benefits strategy.

- **Ensure financial alignment:** Guarantee that your benefits strategy aligns with your overall business objectives.

The second, more detailed, version of the TBA is a multifaceted process that involves:

- **Data collection:** We gather data from various sources, including claims data, plan documents, vendor contracts, employee surveys, and interviews with key stakeholders.

- **Analysis:** We analyze the data across multiple categories of value, identifying trends, patterns, and areas of concern.

- **Scoring and benchmarking:** We score each category and provide a total program performance score, allowing for benchmarking and tracking progress.

- **Reporting and recommendations:** We present our findings in a clear and concise report, along with actionable recommendations for improvement.

The TBA breaks down the value equation into several key categories, including:

1. **Strategic planning:** How does your benefits program support your human capital strategy and broader business objectives?

2. **Cost control:** Is your company effectively managing its healthcare supply chain?

3. **Employee engagement:** Are your employees using the benefits you're investing in?

4. **Employee satisfaction:** Do your employees like and appreciate the benefits you offer?

5. **Benefits administration:** Is your HR team using technology to reduce administrative work and complexity?

6. **Benefits compliance:** Is your organization keeping up with federal and state laws?

7. **Broker performance:** Does your broker know what they're doing, and are they financially incentivized to help you achieve your goals?

The TBA is not just a one-time assessment. It's a recurring process that has become the cornerstone of our approach at Health Compass Consulting. It's how we ensure that our clients get the most value from their benefits programs and achieve their financial and organizational goals.

You can quickly get a sense of how your program is performing by scanning the QR code below or going to https://assessment.healthcompassconsulting.com/fixinghealthcaretba and taking the assessment.

Once complete, you'll get instant feedback and a report sent to your inbox with tailored recommendations on how to improve your scores.

Take the assessment now, and then continue reading.

Next, we'll focus specifically on the health plan component of your benefits package by introducing you to the Health Plan Maturity Model™ (HPMM). This serves as a strategic roadmap for long-term optimization, aligning the progress of your health plans with the natural stages of your company's development.

The Health Plan Maturity Model (HPMM)™

If you think of the TBA as a detailed health checkup for your overall benefits program, the HPMM is your multiyear fitness plan to keep your health plan in peak physical condition, optimizing value right alongside the natural evolution of your company. Just as companies go through distinct phases of development, from startup to maturity, so too should their health plans. The HPMM helps you visualize and navigate this journey, ensuring your health plan evolves in step with your business.

The Health Plan Maturity Model is a framework that outlines the distinct stages of strategic sophistication in managing and optimizing your health plan, mirroring the lifecycle of a company. As such, it's a multiyear roadmap, not a quick fix. This model helps you visualize the journey from basic, often reactive, health plan management to a highly strategic, optimized approach that not only controls costs but also enhances employee health outcomes and significantly increases your company's valuation and long-term stability.

This model is particularly crucial for companies thinking about their long-term future, including a potential sale or acquisition, but also for anyone focused on sustainable growth and increased employee well-being.

I've developed maturity models for each market segment, and each stage of the HPMM represents a higher level of optimization, which results in higher EBITDA, higher employee retention, and a more valuable company.

Although your company can move through the model as fast or slow as you want, accelerating your company's progression increases earnings and the value of your organization.

Health Plan
Maturity Model™
From Health Compass Consulting

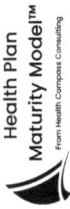

Groups with 1,000–10,000 enrolled employees

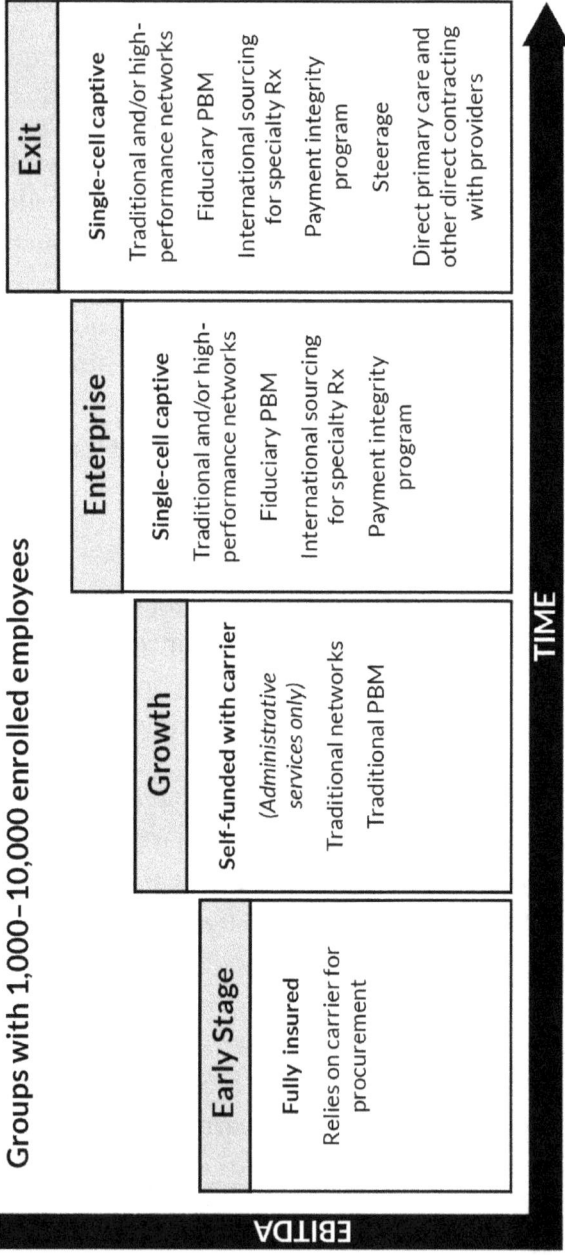

Early Stage	Growth	Enterprise	Exit
Fully insured	Self-funded with carrier	Single-cell captive	Single-cell captive
Relies on carrier for procurement	*(Administrative services only)*	Traditional and/or high-performance networks	Traditional and/or high-performance networks
	Traditional networks	Fiduciary PBM	Fiduciary PBM
	Traditional PBM	International sourcing for specialty Rx	International sourcing for specialty Rx
		Payment integrity program	Payment integrity program
			Steerage
			Direct primary care and other direct contracting with providers

EBITDA

TIME

1. Early stage

In this initial stage, health plan management is primarily reactive to immediate needs, much like any new company operation. Issues are addressed as they arise, often in a hurried and piecemeal fashion. Decisions are largely driven by immediate cost concerns or urgent employee needs, with little or limited long-term planning, similar to how a startup focuses on day-to-day survival.

Data analysis is minimal. The organization, being in its early days, lacks a clear understanding of health plan utilization, cost drivers, and ongoing employee health needs. The focus is on simply providing basic coverage to meet legal requirements, not on optimizing value or employee health, just as a startup focuses on getting off the ground by establishing the basics. This stage is characterized by high costs, low employee satisfaction, and a lack of strategic direction, much like the growing pains of an immature business. Companies at this stage are likely overpaying for care by around $4,000 per employee, per year.

2. Growth stage

In the growth stage, the organization focuses on ensuring the health plan complies with regulations such as ERISA and the ACA and transitions from a "fully insured" funding model to a commoditized, partially self-funded model known as "administrative services only" (ASO). The new funding model provides better claims reporting, and, for the first time, the organization gets a "glimpse" of its healthcare supply chain. For the first time, employers can see what healthcare services their employees are buying and how much they cost the company. This newfound visibility opens up a world of opportunities. Benefits professionals can better identify when patients make poor purchasing decisions or are being overcharged for services. They can also see what specific clinical needs and potential gaps exist within your unique population. These insights not only create short-term opportunities, but this data also makes it easier for underwriters to more accurately price your company's plans. As a result, your company is now in a position to more confidently progress through the maturity model and deliver more value to stakeholders. At this stage, your organization is likely overpaying for care by around $3,000 per employee, per year.

3. Enterprise stage

At the enterprise stage, the organization begins to develop a more bespoke solution for its population. It views its health plan as a strategic asset that can impact employee productivity, retention, and the company's overall financial health. It may further optimize risk-management solutions by creating its own fronting carrier via the use of a "single-cell" captive. Data analysis also becomes more prominent. Through the use of a third-party administrator (TPA), the organization gains access to a more detailed level of claims data, and this provides more insights on how its supply chain can be optimized. In my experience, executives who reach this stage are often shocked to see how much the price of commoditized healthcare services (ie, imaging) varies within a specific market. They ask questions like, "Why are we paying $6,000 for MRIs at this location when we can get them for $600 over here?" While unsettling at first, their visibility into how "screwed up" things actually are inspires them to continue progressing through the model in pursuit of value. Inherently, this visibility opens the door to the concept of "steerage," where plans incentivize and reward members for making value-driven purchasing decisions. The enterprise stage is about building a foundation for long-term success and demonstrating a commitment to strategic health plan management aligned with the focus of a mature business. At the enterprise stage, your organization is probably saving around $2,000 per employee, per year, but you're likely still overpaying for care by around $2,000 per employee, per year.

4. Exit stage

At the exit stage, health plans have reached near peak optimization. The organization has full visibility into its healthcare supply chain and is actively seeking value. In simple terms, it knows the unit prices of hospitalizations, surgeries, labs, imaging, and drugs, and is using this data to get the most value for employees—at the lowest price. Advanced analytics and predictive modeling are used to optimize plan performance, manage risk, and improve employee health outcomes. There is a strong emphasis on value-based care, direct contracting, and innovative solutions that drive quality, efficiency, and cost savings. Employee engagement is high, with personalized communication, tailored resources, and proactive support for health and well-being. At this phase of its life, the company actively manages its relationships with vendors, ensures financial alignment, and continuously monitors and refines its health plan for maximum value and readiness for what happens next, reflecting the optimized and strategic approach of a legacy company. At this stage, your company has done a lot to maximize the return on its benefits but may still be leaving a little profit on the table.

Knowing where your organization stands on the Health Plan Maturity Model is crucial, especially when considering long-term value, a potential exit strategy, and the natural evolution of your company, because it:

- **Aligns with business growth:** It helps synchronize your health plan strategy with your company's overall lifecycle and strategic objectives.

- **Demonstrates strategic foresight:** A mature health plan signals to potential buyers or investors that the company and its management team are focused on driving long-term, sustainable value.

- **Reduces financial risk:** Optimized health plans minimize waste, control costs, and improve employee health, all of which reduce financial risk and increase valuation and stability.

- **Enhances employee productivity and retention:** A strong health plan contributes to a healthy, engaged, and loyal workforce, which is a valuable asset in any acquisition or for long-term growth.

- **Improves due diligence:** A well-documented and optimized health plan makes the due diligence process smoother and faster, increasing the likelihood of a successful transaction and smooth transition

Moving along the Health Plan Maturity Model, from startup to exit, is a strategic journey that requires time, effort, and a long-term perspective, just like growing a successful business in itself. It's about building a valuable asset that not only benefits your employees but also enhances your company's overall worth and stability.

CASE STUDY: Optimizing benefits with a second opinion

The Seminole Education Association (SEA) sought to ensure its district's 10,000 employees received the maximum value from its health plan. Challenged by rising costs, the union contacted my firm (Health Compass Consulting) for a second opinion on their current plan and direction. In it, we conducted a comprehensive review based on the TBA, HPMM, and APIM frameworks shared earlier in this chapter.

This independent review identified potential areas for optimization. As Judy Ngying, Past Vice President of SEA, stated, "We needed to be absolutely certain we were doing right by our members. A second opinion and expert guidance were essential."

Through a collaborative process, we worked closely with SEA leadership to understand their specific needs and priorities. Analysis revealed an opportunity to enhance the efficiency of their PBM strategy, and my firm recommended that SEA push for a new PBM.

The district's procurement process resulted in a new PBM that saved it, its employees, and taxpayers approximately $3.6 million the following year.

Ms. Nyging later noted that, "This money will now be available to fund raises for our teachers, bus drivers, and all education support professionals." The successful collaboration between SEA and Health Compass Consulting demonstrates the power of fiduciary advice and an analytical approach when maximizing value for members.

CASE STUDY: Mark Cuban challenges the industry

Mark Cuban has emerged as one of the most unexpected and disruptive voices challenging the status quo in healthcare. Through the launch of his Cost Plus Drug Company, Cuban put into action many of the same principles discussed in this book: transparency, fairness, and radical elimination of wasteful intermediary costs.

His efforts offer a tangible case study in how bold leadership can expose inefficiencies and realign an industry more closely with the people it is supposed to serve.

The pharmaceutical supply chain, much like the broader healthcare benefits ecosystem, is riddled with hidden markups, opaque pricing structures, and unnecessary intermediary costs. Unlike the brokerage industry, which was developed to serve as retail distribution for health insurers and, by proxy, hospitals, Pharmacy Benefit Managers (PBMs) were initially created by pharmacists in the 1960s to help insurers manage prescription drug plans. However, by 1972, the dynamic flipped when the drug wholesaler McKesson purchased the PBM conglomerate PCS. In 1993, PCS was acquired by drugmaker Eli Lilly, marking a significant shift in this vertical integration. Instead of helping employers manage prescription drug supply chains and maximize value, PBMs now worked for drugmakers, creating yet another misaligned incentive that plagues many employers to this day.

Rather than securing the lowest possible price for end-users, major PBMs frequently generate profits by marking up the price of drugs by undisclosed amounts (ie, "spread pricing"), rebate schemes, and exclusive product placement deals—all things that outrageously drive costs up rather than down.[31] Most consumers

31   K. Martin, *What Pharmacy Managers Do, and How They Contribute to Drug Spending* (The Commonwealth Fund, 2025), www. commonwealthfund.org/publications/explainer/2025/mar/what-pharmacy-benefit-managers-do-how-they-contribute-drug-spending, accessed June 15, 2025

have little understanding of how these mechanisms work because, as we discussed in Chapter 3, the legacy brokers they rely on for guidance profit from their ignorance.

NOTE

The "medical loss ratio" rules in the Affordable Care Act incentivized health insurers to vertically integrate. Since then, major insurers have acquired PBMs, and by 2022, more than half of the profits of major insurers were derived from selling drugs to employers and their employees.[32]

Cuban, however, did recognize this dysfunction and took steps to bypass it entirely. He launched his straightforward, highly transparent Cost Plus Drug Company, which buys generic medications directly from manufacturers and sells them on to consumers with a fixed markup of just 15% plus a pharmacy service fee. There are no hidden rebates and no secret backdoor deals. In an industry seemingly built on smoke and mirrors, this level of radical transparency was—and remains—nothing short of revolutionary.

By stripping away the layers of complexity and obfuscation, Cuban has demonstrated just how

---

32 W. Potter, "Big insurance 2022: Revenues reached $1.25 trillion thanks sucking billions out of the pharmacy supply chain – and taxpayers' pockets", Health Care Un-covered (February 27, 2023), www.linkedin.com/posts/wendell-potter_big-insurance-2022-revenues-reached-125-activity-7036058265582981121-E1Wg/?trk=public_profile_like_view, accessed June 15, 2025

inflated drug prices have become under the traditional model. In many cases, he can offer medication at prices 80% to 90% lower than traditional insurance structures. These stark contrasts make it incredibly difficult for defenders of the traditional model to argue that the current system serves patients' best interests.

Beyond simply offering cheaper medications, Cuban's company is setting a new standard for what ethical healthcare commerce ought to look like. It makes its entire pricing structure available for anyone interested, publicly listing manufacturing costs, the company's 15% markup, and the associated pharmacy fee. There is no guesswork, no fine print. Patients know exactly what they are paying for and why. In doing so, Cuban is not only saving individuals and families hundreds or even thousands of dollars per year, he is also proving a larger point: that the healthcare industry's complexity is not inherent or inevitable.

Cuban's impact extends beyond consumer savings. His model has started to ripple through the broader healthcare economy, pressuring PBMs, insurers, and even some pharmaceutical manufacturers to reconsider their own pricing and contracting strategies. While the entrenched players have significant resources and regulatory tools at their disposal, they can no longer ignore the growing chorus of employers, policymakers, and patients demanding similar transparency and accountability. Cuban's intervention has helped crystallize a central truth: the only reason healthcare costs remain outrageously high is because it serves the financial interests of those who control the current system.

Mark Cuban's model holds critical lessons. Employers have long accepted whatever pharmacy benefits their brokers or insurers packaged for them, often with minimal direct understanding of the embedded costs. Cuban's work demonstrates that there are viable alternatives to taking intermediaries at their word. Employers no longer have to rely on traditional PBM contracts full of opaque rebates and vague promises. Instead, they can explore partnerships with a newer breed of fiduciary-based PBMs, direct contracting strategies, or carve-out programs that separate pharmacy benefits from traditional insurance carriers altogether.

Moreover, Cuban's approach reinforces a key theme emphasized throughout this book: leaders can take ownership of their healthcare purchasing decisions. Delegating benefits management to conflicted brokers or blindly trusting long-standing vendors is no longer defensible. Leadership requires scrutinizing the incentives of every player in the system, demanding full visibility into pricing, and being willing to challenge long-standing assumptions about what is "normal" in healthcare costs.

Cuban's entry into healthcare also illustrates the importance of simplicity. Cost Plus Drugs' model is not built on some breakthrough technological innovation; it simply cuts out unnecessary layers and prioritizes honesty over gamesmanship. In a sector famous for justifying inflated costs with complicated actuarial formulas and jargon, the power of straightforward, common-sense solutions cannot be overstated. Cuban proves that fixing healthcare often isn't about inventing something new, it's about removing what never needed to be there in the first place.

Critically, Cuban's work also shows that change can be both morally and financially profitable. While margins are slim compared to traditional PBMs or specialty pharmacies, the company is rapidly growing and gaining loyalty among a wide swath of the public. In a marketplace increasingly skeptical of large institutions, trust has become a form of currency—and Cuban is earning it by practicing what so few others have: transparency and fairness.

Of course, one entrepreneur alone, even one as talented as Cuban, cannot solve all of the U.S.'s healthcare problems. Many medications, especially specialty drugs and biologics, remain expensive and complex to source. Hospital pricing, surgical procedures, diagnostic imaging—these areas remain dominated by opaque, conflicted pricing models that still cry out for disruption. Yet Cuban's case demonstrates that it is possible, through hard work and passion, to build sustainable healthcare business models that align with consumers' interests, without sacrificing profitability or scalability.

In many ways, Mark Cuban's challenge to the healthcare industry mirrors the challenge I lay before you: stop accepting complexity as an excuse. Stop tolerating opaque vendor relationships. Stop assuming that healthcare waste is inevitable. Cuban's success reminds us that change starts with leadership—leadership willing to question, to innovate, and to reject the cozy relationships that perpetuate dysfunction. Transparency like his is not a luxury or a public relations strategy, it is genuinely transformative. Simplicity is not naïve—it is powerful. Ethical stewardship of healthcare dollars is not incompatible with growth—it is the foundation for it.

Through his work, Cuban has pinpointed issues such as hidden fees and opaque pricing that contradicted his core values. In search of unbiased advice, he ultimately made the bold decision to terminate his broker and take on the task of overhauling his company's health plans in-house. In this capacity, he aimed to construct an employee benefits program from scratch, using the company's distinct position within the pharmaceutical industry to drive down costs.

This strategy was more than just a quest for savings; it was an effort to ensure that the company's internal practices aligned with its external mission. Cuban's actions illustrated that an alternative approach to healthcare benefits, anchored in transparency and affordability, was indeed feasible.

His message to CEOs across the country is unmistakable: the outdated reliance on conflicted vendors for guidance and services is no longer acceptable. He has urged employers to hire someone in a leadership role who has deep expertise in the domain of healthcare financing and procurement so that they can circumvent the conflicts of interest, mitigate fiduciary risk, and create value.

Key takeaways

- What gets measured gets improved.

- Tools like the Total Benefits Assessment score organizations in key categories of benefits value, help them identify opportunities, and track progress over time.

Action items

- See where your organization stands in the Health Plan Maturity Model (HPMM) by going to www. fixinghealthcare.com/hpmm or scanning the QR code below.

- Take the Total Benefits Assessment™ (TBA) to identify opportunities for improvement, then review your scores with qualified benefits professionals.

- To get your score, scan the QR code below, or go to: https://assessment.healthcompassconsulting. com/fixinghealthcaretba

SIX

Building Your Benefits Dream Team—Establishing Selection Criteria

I n Chapter 4, we discussed the virtue of bringing benefits expertise in-house or partnering with external firms. Now, let's delve into the specifics of building your "Benefits Dream Team" by establishing clear criteria for selecting the right in-house professionals or external partners. This chapter will provide a framework for identifying the qualifications, expertise, and alignment necessary to optimize your benefits program and fulfill your fiduciary responsibilities.

Remember: if you are not an expert in employee benefits, you are legally required to engage those who are. This is not optional. Failing to do so can expose your organization to significant liability.

A key consideration when establishing an in-house benefits team is the cost of expertise. You will need to weigh the salary and benefits of an in-house benefits professional against the potential return on investment. A qualified professional can generate a substantial ROI. Depending on your group size and current benefits program, a skilled expert on a typical salary should generate an ROI of 3:1 or even as high as 40:1. This means that, for every dollar spent on salary, you could see a return of $3 to $40 in cost savings.

As a general rule of thumb, I suggest that companies with fewer than 1,000 employees outsource benefits services to an external firm.

Criteria for selecting in-house experts

When recruiting in-house benefits professionals, consider the following criteria:

1. **Credentials and expertise:**

   - **Certified Employee Benefit Specialist (CEBS) designation:** You can think of this designation from the International Association of Employee Benefits Plans as a "bachelor's degree" in benefits. Half of this curriculum focuses on health and welfare plans, and the other half focuses on retirement plans, which you likely need support for as well. There are

over 14,000 benefits professionals with this
certification.

- **Registered Employee Benefits Consultant
  (REBC) designation:** You can think of this
  designation from the National Association
  of Benefits and Insurance Professionals
  (NABIP) as a "master's degree," as it signifies
  a high level of knowledge and expertise in
  employee benefits. With only about 500 REBCs
  in the country, finding one demonstrates a
  commitment to excellence.

- **Certified Health Value Professional (CHVP)
  designation:** For larger companies aiming
  for advanced HPMM strategies, consider
  candidates with both REBC and CHVP
  designations from the Validation Institute. The
  CHVP curriculum offers some of the leading
  education in health plan innovation and can be
  considered equivalent to a Ph.D. in this field.
  With approximately 50 CHVPs in the market,
  this distinction sets candidates apart.

2. **Experience:** While degrees and certifications are
   helpful, there is no substitute for experience in
   this area. To that end, candidates should have at
   least ten years of industry experience and a solid
   understanding of level-funded, self-funded, and
   unbundled self-funded health plans. While many
   benefits professionals have experience with
   traditional bundled products (ie, fully insured,
   bundled level-funded, and ASO products), a

much smaller number actually know how to build and manage health plans from the ground up. Progressing upward through the Health Plan Maturity Model requires a much higher level of expertise, so be on the lookout for professionals who have experience in this area.

3. **Specific skills:**

   - **Analytical skills:** Ability to analyze data, identify trends, and make data-driven decisions.

   - **Negotiation skills:** Experience negotiating with vendors and insurance carriers.

   - **Communication skills:** Strong written and verbal communication skills to effectively convey complex information to stakeholders and employees.

   - **Compliance knowledge:** Deep understanding of ERISA, ACA, and other relevant regulations.

Criteria for selecting fiduciary-based firms

When partnering with a fiduciary-based management consulting firm, consider the following criteria:

1. **Fee-based model:** By definition, fiduciary-based firms cannot accept and keep compensation from vendors associated with health plans. Per their

contractual terms with you, compensation from vendors must be credited back to you, the plan sponsor. This model eliminates conflicts of interest and ensures their advice is aligned with your best interests. In short, this model enables them to serve as a fiduciary to you.

- For more guidelines on this topic, visit www. validationinstitute.com

2. **Clear processes and services:** The firm should have well-defined processes for assessment, procurement, implementation, and management (APIM). They should be able to articulate their services clearly and provide a detailed scope of work. This helps you evaluate the "reasonableness" of their fees and avoid potential service gaps.

3. **Highly credentialed and experienced staff:** Look for firms with consultants who hold the CEBS, REBC, CHVP designations and have significant experience with alternative funding arrangements as described above.

4. **Fiduciary validation:** Seek out firms that have earned the "Fiduciary Validation" from the Validation Institute. This validation indicates that the firm's revenue model aligns with employers' goals and can, therefore, serve as a fiduciary to you. This validation comes with a $100,000 credibility guarantee from the Validation Institute and may reduce the price of your Directors & Officers (D&O) insurance.

5. **Market access:** If you're fully replacing your broker with a fiduciary-based firm, your new firm will need to implement and manage the products you purchase. To do that, your firm needs to be appointed by the insurers you are using. That being said, you'll want to confirm which carriers they have the authority to work with. As you progress through the HPMM, this becomes less and less important, but if your plan is fully insured, these details are critically important.

NOTE

Some fiduciary-based firms opt not to be appointed by major carriers, and others have had appointments terminated as they did not align with the insurers' partnership expectations.

---

6. **Transparency:** By definition, fiduciary-based firms must disclose all fees, and potential conflicts of interest in their contract with you. As an executive, you may be shocked to know that many of you do not have a contract with your current broker. That's a problem.

Evaluation tools

The scoring method such as the one illustrated below, makes it easy to identify the resources best suited for your company.

Here's the general process:

1. Identify at least three fiduciary-based benefits consulting firms for evaluation.

2. Vet and disqualify firms for any of the following reasons:

   - The consultant you would be working with does not possess any of the certifications listed below—*ask for proof.*

   - The firm accepts commissions or bonuses from health insurers.

   - The firm cannot access the entire marketplace because its appointment with a health insurer has been terminated and cannot be reinstated.

   - The firm does not contractually disclose all forms of compensation as required by the Consolidated Appropriations Act.

   - The firm does not have the correct errors and omissions policy for consulting on self-funded health plans—*request and review a certificate of their policy.*

3. Using the criteria established below, rate the remaining firms and add up their scores.

Criteria	Firm #1	Firm #2	Firm #3
Certified Health Value Professional (+10 pts)			
Registered Employee Benefits Consultant (+10 pts)			
Certified Employee Benefit Specialist or Health Rosetta (+5 pts)			
The firm has a formal process for continuously vetting vendors and solutions providers (up to 20 pts)			
The firm offers initial risk-free evaluation services (up to 10 pts)			
Pricing and terms (up to +15 pts)			
At least 50% of the firm's clients are on level-funded or self-funded health plans... (up to +20 pts)			
The firm has been "Fiduciary Validated" by the Validation Institute (+10 pts)			
Total scores			

Meet with the highest-ranking firm to discuss possible next steps.

For those seeking deeper guidance on how to proceed with fiduciary-based service, one resource worth exploring is the Nautilus Institute (www.nautilushealth.org). Nautilus is a pioneering initiative developed by Dave Chase and dedicated to building a better foundation for employer-led healthcare reform. Nautilus has established shared standards of excellence across critical areas such as procurement, contracting, plan management, and data governance. Rather than offering theoretical models, Nautilus provides tangible frameworks that promote measurable transparency and empowers businesses to demand more from their suppliers and partners.

As you evaluate resources like Nautilus, it's important to remember that no single firm, advisor, or service model will be a perfect fit for every organization. Employers are all different, they have different risk tolerances, workforce demographics, cultural values, and financial priorities. They operate in different parts of the world. They build and sell different things. Each needs to find a solution that fits a unique set of circumstances.

With this in mind, it is both acceptable and advisable to strategically mix and match service providers, assembling a best-in-class coalition that aligns with your unique goals. The key is ensuring that every partner you select is aligned with your interests, committed to full transparency, and willing to be held accountable to the standards of fiduciary excellence you are establishing. In the new healthcare economy, strategic customization is a hallmark of true leadership.

For example:

- **Broker for basic management services:** You might use a traditional broker for basic implementation and management of your program.

- **Fiduciary-based firm for consulting and procurement:** Engage a fiduciary-based firm for strategic planning, procurement, and complex plan design.

- **In-house teams for plan management:** Use your in-house team for employee communication, care navigation, and overall program management.

Even with a strong in-house team, partnering with a fiduciary-based firm for specialized projects or ongoing consultation can be beneficial. They can provide an objective perspective and bring fresh ideas to the table.

Comparing common scopes of services offered

Service	Scope	Common legacy brokers	Management consultants
Consulting	Services are ERISA compliant	No	Yes
	Provides formal discovery process	No	Yes
	Quantifies program performance	No	Yes
	Develops multiyear strategy	No	Yes
Procurement	Services are ERISA compliant	No	Yes
	Request for proposal (RFP) sent every year	No	Yes
	# of proposals generated	4–5	12–15
	Develops custom solutions	No	Yes
	Provides strategic recommendations	Maybe	Yes
Management	Implements new programs	Yes	Yes
	Integrates vendors with technology	Yes	Yes
	Monitors performance via dashboard	No	Yes
	Develops full management calendar	No	Maybe
	Processes enrollment changes	Maybe	Maybe
	Manages program compliance	Maybe	Maybe
	Resolves employee service requests	Maybe	Maybe
	Provides ongoing employee education	Maybe	Maybe

Building your Benefits Dream Team requires careful consideration and a clear understanding of your organization's needs. It's the combination of alignment, certified expertise, and formalized processes that empowers businesses to reduce their annual healthcare spend by as much as $4,000 or $5,000 per employee per year—while improving coverage and care for employees.

By using the criteria and scoring methods outlined in this chapter, you can confidently select the right professionals and firms to build benefits programs that truly deliver value to stakeholders.

Key takeaways

- Executives can and should take control of their benefits program.

- Establishing clear criteria for identifying benefits resources is essential for success.

- Fiduciary-based benefits firms can serve as unconflicted partners and typically provide more comprehensive benefits services without adding additional costs.

Action items

- Explore the feasibility of hiring a Chief Benefits Officer or bringing more benefits expertise in-house.

- Research and vet fiduciary-based management consulting firms.

- Visit the Validation Institute's website at www. validationinstitute.com for a list of fiduciary validated management consulting firms.

SEVEN

Switching To A Fiduciary-Based Firm

Throughout this book, we have emphasized a fundamental truth: traditional, commission-driven benefits models are failing U.S. businesses. Employers are wasting billions of dollars through misaligned incentives, lack of transparency, and outdated procurement models that prioritize brokers' interests over their clients'. A fiduciary-based benefits firm, however, offers a bold, independent alternative, one that prioritizes your organization's financial health and your employees' well-being. But recognizing the need for change is only one step. The real challenge lies in the transition itself. When and how should you make the switch? What obstacles might arise? How do you ensure the change delivers the strategic benefits management revolution your business needs?

In this final chapter, I explore the answers to these questions. I offer advice based on my personal experience from both sides of the fence to help you transition from a legacy system that is costing you dearly to a fiduciary-based model that challenges the status quo.

Up to this point, we've discussed the need for a shift to fiduciary-based benefits firms. Now, let's examine a concrete example of why this change is so crucial. Often, change in business is unexpected, and it's precisely in these moments that the weaknesses of legacy brokers become apparent. Their priorities can be misaligned, turning change into a chance for them to profit, often to the detriment of the employer. This next case study vividly illustrates this dynamic.

CASE STUDY: Avoiding an unexpected 34% rate hike

In 2024, Bluewave Resource Partners, a thriving recruiting and staffing firm with 200 professionals nationwide, faced a daunting challenge. Their existing health insurer, Humana, abruptly exited the market, leaving them and their broker scrambling for alternatives. Their legacy broker, operating under a traditional commission-based model, requested proposals from traditional health insurers and presented what it thought was the best option: a 34%

rate increase from a publicly traded health insurer. This would skyrocket Bluewave's per employee per year (PEPY) costs from $6,221 to $8,336, threatening profit margins and employee morale. This scenario is all too common, where businesses are presented with limited options and inflated costs due to the "brokerage blind spot"—a system rife with hidden commissions and misaligned incentives. Bluewave's situation highlighted a critical issue: were they receiving truly unbiased advice, or were their options limited by their broker's compensation structure and narrow understanding of healthcare financing and procurement?

Bluewave's experience exemplified the opaque conflicts of interest inherent in traditional brokerage models. Their legacy broker, compensated as a percentage of premiums and year-end bonuses based on total volumes of business with each carrier, had a financial incentive to maintain or even increase costs. The limited options they presented raised a red flag. Were those options truly the best for Bluewave, or simply the most profitable for the broker? This is where MDI becomes problematic. When carrier commissions and bonus programs incentivize brokers, their advice can be compromised. Bluewave's CEO, Charlie Lewis, and newly appointed President, Laura Danforth, recognized this conflict and understood it was time for a change.

Bluewave sought a partner who prioritized their interests above all else—a fiduciary. Health Compass Consulting, operating on a transparent, fee-based model, was engaged to provide unbiased advice and strategic benefits management. At Health Compass, we operate with a mission to eliminate wasteful healthcare spending, driven by a fiduciary business model free from the typical conflicted carrier compensation models. We applied our APIM™ (Assess, Procure, Implement, Manage) Framework to transform Bluewave's benefits program:

- **Assess:** To develop a baseline and properly diagnose the problem, we conducted a thorough analysis of Bluewave's current plan, employee demographics, and financial goals. Through the TBA framework, we evaluated the company's health and welfare programs across seven key categories of value, enabling them to identify opportunities for improvement. From there, we worked with their team to set goals and develop roadmaps to achieve them.

- **Procure:** Instead of just getting proposals from the same three to five health insurers Bluewave had been shown for years, we aimed to give the company much broader visibility into the marketplace of healthcare strategies and solutions. To achieve this, we negotiated proposals with over twelve health insurers, using various funding and risk-management techniques. We also explored several bespoke solutions, and one of them helped the company progress from the "early" to "enterprise" stage of the Health Plan Maturity Model™. While keeping PEPY costs virtually flat at $6,256, the customized health plan tremendously increased provider access and maintained existing coverage levels. We also introduced employee incentives, including $0 out-of-pocket costs for high-quality surgery centers, virtual acute care options, and prescription drug savings through a fiduciary-based PBM.

- **Implement:** To ensure employees understood how to maximize the value of their new plan, we held several educational webinars and facilitated one-on-one coaching sessions, allowing them to discuss their more personal health needs. We also managed the contracting process with vendors supporting the health plan, and assisted the company in developing a sustainable and equitable contribution strategy.

- **Manage:** We developed a monthly benefits management calendar, which served as a checklist to clarify administrative and compliance tasks that needed to be executed and assigned responsibilities. Since Bluewave's new plan provided detailed claims-data, this newfound transparency allowed us to monitor the plan's performance and identify cost-saving opportunities on an ongoing basis, which we discussed at our quarterly benefit review (QBR) meetings.

We began guiding Bluewave through the Health Plan Maturity Model™ (HPMM), a strategic framework for optimizing benefits programs. By progressing through the stages of HPMM, Bluewave transitioned from a reactive approach to a proactive, data-driven funding strategy, ensuring that the company only paid for healthcare services used by employees and enabling the plan to spend less on costly prescription drugs. This alignment ensured that their benefits program matched their business growth and long-term objectives.

The result avoided the 34% rate increase, enhanced engagement, and reduced risk. The new benefits strategy delivered significant results for Bluewave:

- **Cost containment:** By avoiding the 34% rate increase, Bluewave saved $2,075 per employee, a substantial financial impact.

- **Seamless transition:** Health Compass Consulting managed the transition to the new carrier, minimizing disruption and simplifying administration.

- **Employee engagement:** Employee participation increased due to improved provider access, $0 virtual care, and reduced costs for individuals and families.

- **Competitive advantage:** The optimized benefits package strengthened Bluewave's ability to attract and retain top talent.

- **Increased compliance:** Working with a fiduciary firm ensured that Bluewave met ERISA requirements and the Consolidated Appropriations Act (CAA), which requires transparency from benefits firms.

Bluewave's story demonstrates the power of unbiased advice and strategic benefits management. By partnering with a fiduciary, they escaped the brokerage blind spot, reclaimed significant savings, and improved employee satisfaction. As I emphasize throughout this book, businesses can save millions by moving away from conflicted models and embracing transparency and accountability. Bluewave's success proves that with the right approach, organizations can transform their benefits programs from a cost center to a strategic asset.

Avoiding disruption

Assuming you can plan around change, it is crucial to understand that switching benefits firms doesn't alter your existing lines of coverage or your negotiated terms and pricing with vendors. Your relationships with insurance carriers, third-party administrators (TPAs), pharmacy benefit managers (PBMs), and other vendors can all remain in place. What changes is who advises you, who stands beside you in negotiations, designs your plans, and helps you deliver more value.

To use a picturesque analogy, think of it as changing a ship's navigator mid-way across the ocean. Rather than building a whole new ship and starting again, you're just using new navigational expertise. Regardless of who advises your business, you retain control of your benefits programs, so why not let an expert with a fiduciary obligation steer with your best interests at heart? Such a change in the advisory relationship can yield profound effects over time. A fiduciary-based firm is likely to scrutinize future renewals, challenge vendors to deliver greater value, and develop a long-term benefits strategy rooted in optimizing your total rewards investment. In the short term, however, there's little need to disrupt current plans or cause excessive upheaval.

Importantly, a decision based on what is best for its employees, rather than its broker, is more likely to be perceived as a benefit. This in turn fosters a stronger culture of trust, loyalty, and improved employee retention. Discussed in the right terms, gaining independent advice, cost savings, and increased employee well-being becomes something to celebrate rather than fear. Any concerns about disruption can be navigated by positioning change as a necessary force for good.

Making the switch straightforward

The first practical question when it comes to a planned transition is often "when?" While, technically, you can switch benefits firms at any point during the plan year, there are strategic windows where the switch is smoother, more productive, and more impactful than at other times.

For mid-size employer groups, starting to transition two to three months after your plan's renewal date is ideal. By this time, your annual enrollment is complete, vendor contracts have been renewed or extended, and there is a window of relative calm before the next cycle of benefit planning begins. This is the ideal time to move to a fiduciary firm because, during this window, your new partner can thoroughly assess your benefits program using the TBA or an equivalent. With breathing room and access to historical data and up-to-date information, your new advisor can diagnose inefficiencies, identify savings opportunities, and develop a strategic roadmap tailored to your organization.

Conversely, switching firms within the ninety days leading up to renewal is fraught with complications. Vendors are actively negotiating renewals, plans are being finalized, and administrative tasks such as open enrollment communications are underway. Introducing a transition during this critical window is similar to trying to remodel your kitchen the weekend before Thanksgiving, a stressful process that is unlikely to yield the best outcomes.

Another common pitfall is for employers to run a head-to-head competition between suppliers. Attempting to have two firms run procurement simultaneously might seem sensible; however, this well-meaning strategy can often backfire. Carriers do not offer preferential pricing based on who represents the client. In fact, when carriers receive two RFPs for the same client (a phenomenon known as "dual activity" in the business), they provide each firm with the same exact proposal and stop negotiating.

To optimize your negotiating position, it is advisable to commit fully to a single fiduciary-based advisor. Vendors, like employers, prefer clarity, focus, and decisiveness. Your best outcomes arise when your advisor has a clear mandate to act, unencumbered by competition from a second firm muddying the waters. Having one navigator is the most effective way to avoid getting lost and create a successful benefits transformation.

When it becomes time to switch, there are important considerations to make regarding compensation. According to the Validation Institute's guidelines for Fiduciary Validated Benefits Firms, it is important to instigate a formal "Transition Period." Beginning with the hire date of your new firm and ending the day before your benefits renew, your new fiduciary-based firm is allowed to accept commissions from vendors during this time.

A well-defined transition period is important because it allows you to avoid having to pay twice: commissions to your previous firm and again via direct fees to your new advisor. During this time, transparency is paramount. Your new fiduciary advisor should disclose exactly what commissions are being accepted, from whom, and for how long. Nothing should be hidden or obscured. Once the new plan starts, the books can be balanced and commissions are removed. This transition process solidifies the foundation for a true fiduciary partnership built on trust and transparency.

The onboarding process

A successful transition is largely due to a robust onboarding process. Many employers mistakenly view onboarding as a simple administrative function, focusing on getting paperwork in order, but it is actually a more strategic project. If mishandled, it can undermine the entire transition and, at best, delay the realization of promised benefits. At worst, it can prevent the realization of benefits altogether.

Transitioning to a fiduciary-based firm can be a transformational move for your organization, but success hinges on a disciplined, strategic approach. Based on real-world case studies and industry best practices, I suggest the following are worthy of careful consideration:

- **A thorough assessment:** Your new firm must deeply understand your current plans, vendor relationships, claims experience, employee demographics, cost drivers, and strategic goals. This discovery phase is where inefficiencies are uncovered, hidden fees are exposed, and early opportunities for quick wins are identified. It is a key way in which transitioning to fiduciary-based services differs from broker-based relationships, and I have covered this in detail in preceding chapters.

- **Clear communication channels:** Regular updates, open-door policies for questions, and clear escalation paths for any issues that arise foster trust and eliminate the fear of the unknown. Your team should always feel informed and empowered, not left in the dark.

- **Data collection:** Comprehensive data collection is critical. Plan documents, contracts, vendor agreements, utilization reports, financial statements, and prior audit results should be easily accessible to your new benefits partner. Missing data leads to delays or, worse, the making of assumptions to fill in any gaps. Assumptions are often an enemy of good decision-making, and it is certainly worth assigning a project lead within your organization to oversee the collection and transmission of all necessary data and documentation. Maintaining strict version control will prevent outdated or incomplete information from slowing the transition.

- **Technology integration:** Effective integration between your internal HRIS, payroll systems, and the advisor's technology is imperative. This should include automated data feeds, transparent reporting dashboards, and real-time analytics as standard. It is critical to validate this integration, as relying on assumptions can lead to technology clashes that severely impact professional relationships.

- **Milestones and timelines:** The onboarding plan should define clear timelines, agreed-upon key deliverables, and project milestones that are signposted. Examples include "complete the assessment phase," "deliver initial cost-containment report," "propose new vendor strategy," and "conduct employee feedback survey." The contractual relationship between you and your chosen fiduciary partners is likely to be unique, and, as such, the milestones and timelines will be unique, too. It is important to discuss and agree on desired behaviors and outcomes in a timely and professional manner.

- **Communication with your current broker:** This may, in fact, be the most challenging aspect of a transition. Like most businesses, legacy brokerage firms do not like to lose customers. You need to inform your current broker in a professional, timely, and direct manner, maintaining respect but also not letting their aggressive retention strategies sway your decision.

To keep your transition on track, it is important to set out your expectations explicitly from the outset of all your discussions with potential suppliers: transparency, proactive strategy, measurable savings, enhanced employee satisfaction, and continuous improvement are some of the outcomes available to you, so do not be afraid to ask for them. Remember, companies working in this space, like my own, exist because of a desire to work without conflict solely in our clients' best interests.

Success can, and does, take a little time. It can be challenging to resist the urge for quick fixes and immediate savings that only scratch the surface of what's possible. By committing to a whole new way of working and, in effect, a full, comprehensive strategic overhaul of your benefits plans, you are opening the door to a world of opportunity that's worth waiting for. Maximizing future benefits, however, needs expert consideration, a full assessment of your options, and a long-term view. Patience is a virtue, as are engagement and active leadership. Legacy brokers count on a degree of client apathy and indifference, but fiduciary-based benefits companies thrive with clients who drive accountability, ask questions, and scrutinize deliverables.

Your watchwords should include "trust," of course, but also "verify." Reviewing benchmarks, auditing carrier contracts, and demanding visibility into fees, savings estimates, and ongoing performance are critical parts of fiduciary care. Establishing a sense of partnership, not delegation, is the right mindset when it comes to switching partners. Transformations don't occur by chance. They happen when executive leadership embraces transparency, commits to strategic partnership, and empowers new fiduciary firms to drive meaningful, long-term change.

Anticipating and overcoming challenges

No transition is without its challenges. Yet, anticipating those hurdles is one of the most powerful steps you can take to ensure a smooth and successful shift. Rather than reacting to problems after they arise, a proactive approach allows you to minimize disruption and maintain momentum. Below, I've outlined some of the most common obstacles organizations encounter when transitioning to a fiduciary-based benefits firm, along with practical strategies for navigating them with confidence and clarity:

- **Resistance from legacy brokers:** Expect emotional appeals, "special offers," and fear tactics from your outgoing broker. Stay firm, stay fact-based, and remember why you made the switch.

- **Data transfer delays:** Some former brokers may intentionally delay the release of documents and technology license transfers necessary for a smooth transition. In my experience, these occurrences are rare. Regardless, it's helpful to build extra time into your project plan in case delays become excessive.

- **Vendor confusion:** If you are fully replacing your legacy broker, you will need to assign your new firm "Broker of Record" (BOR). As you're probably aware, this is done by signing a standardized letter for each carrier telling them that your new firm now has the authority to implement, manage, and service your plans on your behalf. Each carrier has its own slight variation to this process, so it's important that you and your new firm plan accordingly.

Bumps in the road are inevitable, but with the combination of proper planning, clear communication, and trust, these obstacles are easily overcome.

Switching to a fiduciary-based partner signals to your employees that you prioritize their health and financial security. It signals to your board or ownership that you are serious about reclaiming waste and driving sustainable growth. Most importantly, it signals to the marketplace that your company is committed to leadership in the new era of corporate responsibility. Done correctly, it unlocks hidden value in your benefits program, fosters greater employee loyalty, drives down costs, and positions you competitively in a tight labor market. It is not without challenges, but the rewards—both financial and organizational—are transformative.

The journey begins with a single decision to demand better, to reject outdated, misaligned, and wasteful legacy broker commission-driven models, and to embrace independent stewardship of your company's interests and employees' well-being.

Let the transformation begin.

Key takeaways

- Switching to a fiduciary-based firm can lead to significant savings and improved outcomes.

- The transition can be minimally disruptive.

- Potential challenges can be anticipated and overcome.

Action items

- Develop a plan for transitioning to fiduciary-based benefits services.

- Communicate the change to your team and stakeholders.

- Prepare for potential challenges and develop mitigation strategies.

Conclusion: My Vision For Economic Opportunity Through Healthcare Reform

We've explored the history and complexities of employee benefits, as well as the significant financial waste that burdens American businesses—a staggering $4,000 per employee per year. This status quo is unsustainable and is undermining your organization's economic potential, as well as your employees' ability to pursue their dreams. However, I believe in the power of transformation. I envision a future where American businesses are freed from runaway healthcare costs, where every benefits dollar is strategically invested in productivity, job creation, and the financial security of our workforce. I picture a nation where families have peace of mind, enabling them to dream bigger, take risks, and contribute fully to our economy and society.

The key to this transformation is reclaiming control, demanding transparency, and embracing a new era of responsibility. It's about moving beyond outdated, commission-driven models and prioritizing both your business's financial health and your employees' well-being through unbiased, fiduciary-based advice.

While benefits professionals are vital to the well-being of organizations, the legacy brokerage model's tangled web of misaligned incentives actually fuels the medical industrial complex's ability to unfairly profit at the expense of employers, employees, and patients. This not only hinders the industry's ability to serve employers effectively, but also tarnishes its reputation, making it harder to attract a new generation of talent, which is increasingly driven by purpose rather than just a paycheck.

A missed opportunity

This is not merely about cost-cutting; it's about unlocking a massive financial opportunity and revitalizing the American economy, empowering our workforce with the stability they need to live inspired lives. It's about restoring the promise of employer-sponsored healthcare as a true benefit that strengthens families and communities. By aligning resources, identifying waste, negotiating better pricing, and helping employees access high-quality care, you can reduce costs while improving coverage for your employees.

It's about leading the way to a more sustainable, equitable, and economically vibrant America, where everyone has the opportunity to thrive.

Fiduciary duty means acting with the utmost trust and loyalty on behalf of another party, and the legacy brokerage industry is failing America because it cannot serve in a fiduciary capacity.

If you're concerned about potential conflicts of interest, lack of transparency, or rising healthcare costs, switching to a fiduciary-based firm can provide you with unbiased advice, strategic guidance, and a greater return on your benefits investment.

The journey to get there begins with a commitment to change, a willingness to question the status quo, and a desire to do better for our businesses and our nation. American businesses have the power to lead this transformation en masse and drive economic opportunity through healthcare reform, giving more Americans the chance to live their best lives, and you can make a difference.

Take the first step

Let's start by shedding light on your employee benefits program's potential to fuel economic growth and personal fulfillment. I invite you to take our Quick Benefits Checkup, the initial version of our TBA. The

TBA is our proprietary methodology for evaluating your benefits program across seven key categories of value. It provides a comprehensive snapshot of your current state, identifies areas for improvement, and establishes a baseline for measuring progress.

The Quick Benefits Checkup just takes five minutes to complete.

Scan the QR code below, or go to: https://assessment. healthcompassconsulting.com/fixinghealthcaretba

After completing the Quick Benefits Checkup, you'll be invited to meet with me or a member of my team to review your scores, identify opportunities for improvement, and receive tailored recommendations on how to improve.

The choice is clear. You can either continue suffering from conflicted advice and losing $4,000 per employee per year in profit, or you can reclaim this profit by fulfilling your fiduciary responsibility.

Here's the six-step process for leading your organization's healthcare transformation:

1. Get unbiased advice.

2. Quantify your current state.

3. Set goals and develop a multi-year strategy.

4. Procure service providers.

5. Implement changes.

6. Manage and optimize.

Investing in a stronger America

By taking control, demanding transparency, and seeking unbiased advice, you can reclaim nearly $4,000 per employee each year, strengthen your organization, and provide your employees with the financial security needed to pursue their dreams.

By fixing healthcare at your organization, you are helping to build a stronger America, and I look forward to partnering with you on this vital mission.

Acknowledgments

To my incredible wife, Emily, and our young kids, Quinton and Abby. Thank you for your patience and for sacrificing precious time with your dad so that this book could finally make its way out of my head and into the hands of those who need it.

None of this is possible without you.

To my mom, affectionately known as "St. Katherine," thank you for instilling in me a solid moral backbone and an unwavering commitment to doing what is right. To my father, Ken, thank you for giving me the courage to speak truth to power; your strength and resilience, especially during the writing of this book, have been an inspiration.

To my brother Brian and my sister-in-law Kate, thank you for letting me complete this book from the living room of your beautiful home on Glimmerglass Lake.

I'd also like to acknowledge a few key individuals who were instrumental in shaping this work:

- Al Lewis, for his invaluable insights and for providing the foreword.

- Darren Fogarty, for his thought leadership.

- David Contorno, for his courage and pioneering work in the field of fee-based benefits consulting.

- Justin Leader, for sharing his expertise and the powerful case study that demonstrates the impact of unbiased advice.

And to the many colleagues who provided guidance, support, and inspiration:

- Vidar Jorgensen

- Dr. Cristin Dickerson

- Joe LaMantia III

- David Smith

- Julie Selesnic

- Emma Fox

- Stephanie Koch

- Jamie Greenleaf

- Jeff Hogan
- Nelson Griswold
- Stacey Richter
- Peter Prosol
- Henry Parker
- Brian Klepper
- Jessica Brooks-Woods
- Heidi Cottle
- Niko Caparisos
- Karen van Caulil
- Lee Lewis
- Jim Downing
- Jim Turney
- Conny Cranford
- Maurice Clarke
- Bunky Garrabrant
- Carol Hensal
- Kate Shockey
- Julie Griffin
- Saru Seshadri
- Judy Ngying

- Brian Klepper

- Ken Peach

- Sean McDermott

- Laura Danforth

- Charlie Lewis

- Andrew Serio

- Dave Chase

- Mike Carter

- George Boue

- Kristen Allen

- Chris Pyle

- Zeev Neuwirth

- David Goldhill

- Joe Gregory and the team at Rethink Press

To my first bosses in the insurance industry, David Leli and Mike Higgins, thank you for believing in me and teaching me the landscape early on... it has helped every step of the way.

Lastly, to the thousands of healthcare providers and benefits professionals who work tirelessly to help the American people, yet too often find themselves constrained by a system that doesn't always support their noble objectives. Your dedication does not go unnoticed.

The Author

Donovan Pyle is the CEO of Health Compass Consulting and author of *Fixing Healthcare: How executives can save their people, their business, and the economy*. He also serves as a senior advisor at the Validation Institute in Boston. Backed by the highest designations in the employee benefits industry, Donovan brings a unique blend of creative vision and analytical rigor to the complex world of healthcare and employee benefits.

While working on the insurer and brokerage side of the industry, Donovan witnessed how the misaligned incentives between brokers and employers significantly undermined the financial and physical health of organizations. To counter the brokerage industry,

Donovan founded Health Compass Consulting in 2018. The pioneering fiduciary-based management consulting firm is dedicated to helping employers with 100 to 10,000 employees combat the estimated $300 billion in annual waste within the U.S. employer-sponsored healthcare system. To achieve this, the firm developed three proprietary frameworks: Assess, Procurement, Implement, Manage™, Total Benefits Assessment™, and the Health Plan Maturity Model™. These frameworks empower clients with the clarity essential for identifying opportunities, setting goals, and developing roadmaps to achieve them. As a result of their data-driven approach and role as fiduciaries, Health Compass Consulting's clients save an average of $1,856 per employee per year, with better coverage.

As Chairman of the Validation Institute's Certified Health Value Professional (CHVP) Advisory Board, Donovan further contributes to the industry by elevating the professional standards of benefits consulting through leading education on health plan innovation.

Donovan's insights on transforming employee benefits from a cost center to a strategic asset are regularly featured in publications such as "Employee Benefit News," "Strategic CHRO," "SHRM," and "Seeking Alpha." He is a frequent speaker at industry events and a contributor to podcasts, offering actionable strategies for executives seeking to improve the financial and physical health of their organizations. He was recognized as the 2025 Benefit Advisor of the Year by the Validation Institute.

For collaborations, please visit:

🌐 www.fixinghealthcare.com and www.donovan-pyle.com

in www.linkedin.com/in/donovanpyle

www.ingramcontent.com/pod-product-compliance
Lightning Source LLC
Chambersburg PA
CBHW050102210326
41519CB00015BA/3790